D0605241

# Successful Microwaving

## with Toshiba

Dear Friends,

We are pleased that you have selected a Toshiba micro-wave oven — your passport to a versatile and innova-tive cooking experience. Your new oven reflects exten-sive research, thoughtful planning and quality design. It offers you the features most wanted by today's busy consumer.

This book combines a collection of carefully tested reci-pes and directions for getting the most out of your new Toshiba microwave oven. You will appreciate the step-by-step approach and numerous full-color pictures to ease your transition into the exciting world of micro-wave cooking.

Before using your oven for the first time, it is important that you read the Owner's Guide. Then, we encourage you to read the information in this book, particularly that preceding the recipe section. You will find numerous tips and suggestions for successful microwaving.

Now, begin your microwave adventure. Cooking has never been so convenient or so enjoyable!

Sincerely,

TOSHIBA CORPORATION
Home Appliance Department

## Precautions To Avoid Possible Exposure To Excessive Microwave Energy

(a) Do not attempt to operate this oven with the door open since open-door operation can result in harmful exposure to microwave energy. It is important not to defeat or tamper with the safety interlocks.

(b) Do not place any object between the oven front face and the door or allow soil or cleaner residue to accumulate on sealing surfaces.

(c) Do not operate the oven if it is damaged. It is particularly important that the oven door close properly and that there is no damage to the: (1) door (bent); (2) hinges and latches (broken or loosened); (3) door seals and sealing surfaces.

(d) The oven should not be adjusted or repaired by anyone except properly qualified service personnel.

# Contents

## Special Features of Your Oven

Toshiba America, Inc. manufactures many microwave oven models, each with distinctive features. Your oven may have some or all of the conveniences referred to in this book. Following is a general description of each feature to assist you in using them with confidence and to maximum advantage. For more information, refer to the Owner's Guide.

**Variable Power Level:** Each recipe calls for a specific power level, the one most appropriate for the food being microwaved. This is similar to oven temperature in conventional cooking. With the microwave oven, simply turn the power level knob to the desired power level number as directed in the recipe. For touch control ovens, just touch the number of the power level. In all recipes, HIGH means full power. NOTE: Some models will automatically read "0" along with the variable power number selected. For example, when ③ is selected, the oven will read "30."

**Temperature Probe:** Toshiba's microwave oven temperature probe automatically performs the same task as a conventional food thermometer. Refer to the meat chart for the desired internal temperature. Then, dial the temperature or set the desired temperature. The probe monitors the food's internal temperature and turns the oven off when that temperature is reached.

**Defrost:** Defrosting requires a lower power level, usually ④, which generates just enough heat to melt ice crystals and defrost the food. Refer to the charts on defrosting for specific information. AUTO DEFROST is a special programmed cycle which gradually reduces the power level as the food defrosts. To convert the times in the defrosting charts for AUTO DEFROST, add the standing time to the microwave time, then set AUTO DEFROST, using the total time.

**HEAT & HOLD:** Some ovens equipped with the temperature probe also have a HEAT & HOLD feature. This cycle cooks foods at a simmer setting or can hold foods at a desired temperature until serving time.

For the recipes in this book which require simmering or slow cooking, HEAT & HOLD may be used. Follow these steps: (1) Place the probe into the liquid in the dish and plug the jack into the oven wall; (2) Touch the HEAT & HOLD pad, then set 180°; (3) Start the oven. The oven will bring the liquid up to 180° and maintain that temperature. Allow the food to simmer for 1½ to 2 hours, or the length of time recommended in recipe. This gentle cooking method is convenient for stews, pot roasts and other recipes which benefit from slow cooking.

## How Microwaves Work

Microwaves are high frequency electromagnetic waves. They are like radio waves, only much shorter — less than 5 inches long.

In your microwave oven, food absorbs microwave energy, causing food molecules to vibrate. The vibration causes friction which produces heat, much like the heat that results from the friction created by rubbing your hands together.

In microwave cooking, the dish used must be transparent to microwaves (glass, pottery, paper and plastic). The energy passes through it and penetrates the food from all directions, causing heat in the areas of penetration. These areas begin to cook, spreading heat through conduction to other parts of the food.

Metal, including the walls of the microwave oven, reflects microwaves. Since microwaves cannot penetrate metal, metal containers are not generally suggested for microwave cooking — they do not allow the energy to be absorbed by all areas of the food.

**Custom Select:** Ovens with Custom Select automatically program the oven for the proper cooking cycle. Code numbers are listed at the top of each recipe where appropriate. Use this code instead of the times in the recipe. Complete details are given in the Owner's Guide.

# Microwave Utensils

Microwave cooking requires utensils made of materials that are transparent to microwaves. Microwave energy passes through the container to heat the food. Because microwaves heat the food, not the container, many utensils and coverings which cannot be used in a conventional oven work well in the microwave. You can heat and serve on a paper plate, and use plastic wrap to create a cover for a dish that doesn't have one.

Pictured above are a variety of microwave-safe utensils. Some are probably ones you already have on hand. Glass, glass ceramic (such as Corningware®), stoneware, pottery, and porcelain containers can all be used for microwave cooking. Paper and some plastics (such as foam and dishwasher-safe containers) can be used for heating food to serving temperature, but will distort or melt after prolonged contact with very hot food.

You can buy many utensils designed specifically for use in the microwave oven, often bearing the label "microwave-oven-safe." Many are designed to arrange foods in a ring, such as round muffin pans and ring-shaped pans for cakes and meatloaves. Microwave roasting racks, like conventional meat roasting racks, elevate meat so it doesn't cook in hot fat and juices.

**Test for microwave-safety.** If you are not sure a utensil is microwave-safe, perform the following test. Place dish in the oven. Measure ½ to 1 cup water in a glass cup and place it on or beside the dish. Microwave for 1 to 2 minutes at HIGH. If the dish remains cool, it is microwave-safe. If the dish becomes warmer than the water, it should not be used in the oven.

## Utensils *(continued)*

**Do not use** dishes, pans or other containers that are made of metal or have metal handles or trim. Metal pans reflect microwave energy and do not allow it to pass through and heat the food. Also avoid using paper-covered wire twist ties, some types of dinnerware, such as Centura® or Melamine®, conventional meat and candy thermometers, and foil-lined packages. Foil trays under ¾ inch deep can be used, although heating will occur only on the exposed top surface. Keep foil at least 1 inch from oven walls.

## *Utensil Size and Shape*

**Round shapes** allow food to microwave evenly because the energy penetrates equally from all directions. Square and rectangular pans allow microwaves to penetrate corners from both sides, often resulting in overcooking. Corners may require shielding to prevent this.

**Depth** has considerable impact on cooking time. A shallow casserole with a 2-qt. capacity will take less time to microwave than a deeper casserole with the same capacity. More food surface is exposed in the shallow container and cooking time is shortened.

**Ring shapes** work well for foods which cannot be stirred during cooking. This shape allows energy to penetrate food from the center as well as from the sides, top and bottom. Cooking is faster and more even.

**Straight-sided dishes** keep the depth of food uniform so food cooks more evenly. Avoid using containers with sloping sides, in which shallower areas can overcook.

# Suitable Coverings

**Glass covers** help retain steam and speed cooking. Use this type of cover when steaming foods which require little or no added moisture, such as vegetables. Glass covers can become hot during cooking, so handle carefully. A plate can substitute for a glass cover.

**Plastic wrap** forms a snug cover that retains steam for quick cooking. It doubles as a dish when wrapped tightly around whole, moist foods like an ear of corn or a head of cauliflower. Plastic wrap is a good substitute for a glass cover. To prevent splitting, make a steam vent by turning back one edge slightly.

**Wax paper** forms a loose cover that holds in heat, speeds cooking and prevents spatters. Use it when a moist, but not steamed result is desired. To avoid melting the wax paper, make sure it doesn't touch the food during cooking.

**Glass cover with wax paper** creates a tighter fit when cover is loose-fitting. Place a sheet of wax paper between casserole and lid to retain more steam and heat, and reduce moisture evaporation.

**Cooking bags** hold in steam to tenderize larger cuts of meat. Tie bag loosely with string or piece of plastic cut from the open end of the bag, leaving a small space for steam to escape. Place bag in glass baking dish.

**Paper towels** help absorb excess moisture to keep bread surfaces dry. They provide a light covering which retains some steam and prevents spattering. Do *not* use recycled paper in the microwave.

# How Water, Fat, Sugar and Salt React to Microwaving

Water, fat, sugar and salt attract microwave energy, affecting the cooking results of foods containing those ingredients. Here's what to watch for when microwaving such foods.

**Water** attracts microwave energy, causing foods with a high-moisture content to microwave well. Add very little water when cooking high moisture foods such as fresh and frozen vegetables. Too much added water attracts energy away from food and slows cooking.

**Fat** can attract energy away from the meat and slow cooking. Choose well-marbled roasts or ground meat, and trim away large areas of fat. Large cuts of meat will brown as fat rises to the surface during the longer cooking time.

**Sugar** attracts microwave energy, causing high-sugar areas of food (such as frostings, sweet fillings and glazes) to heat more quickly than the remaining area. Avoid overheating these high-sugar areas.

**Salt**, when sprinkled on a food before microwaving, may cause burned spots to occur wherever the salt granules lie. To avoid this, dissolve the salt in a little water and pour over the food, or salt after microwaving is completed.

# Factors to Consider When Microwaving

When choosing foods, preparation methods, containers and cooking times for microwaving, several factors should be considered. The more you cook with your microwave, the easier it will be for you to make choices that will produce successful results.

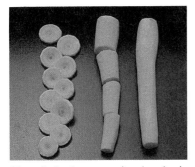

**Size**. In both conventional and microwave cooking, small pieces cook more quickly than large. For even cooking, cut food into pieces of uniform size.

**Container size and shape**. Choose round and ring-shaped dishes for even cooking. Food microwaved in a shallow container will cook more quickly than in a deeper container of the same capacity.

**Density**. Foods with heavy textures take longer to microwave than foods with porous, airy textures. A brownie will take longer to heat than a piece of bread.

**Quantity**. Small amounts cook more quickly than large amounts. When you increase the quantity of food, you must also increase the microwaving time.

**Moisture content**. Foods with high natural moisture microwave best with minimal added water. Too much added moisture slows cooking. Foods with low moisture content do not microwave well.

**Doneness**. Microwaved foods continue to cook after removal from the oven. Some foods may look partially cooked after microwaving, but will complete cooking during the standing time. Check for doneness after the minimum cooking time.

**Foods which do not microwave well** include those with a very low moisture content and those which need dry heat for crisp or crusty results, like popovers and double crust pies. Do *not* use the microwave for canning, deep-fat frying or cooking eggs in the shell.

# Food Placement

Placement in the oven affects the way food cooks. Foods with uneven shapes and thicknesses require special placement for even cooking. The guidelines below will help you determine how to place unevenly shaped foods to insure even cooking.

**Center** smaller areas and thinner parts of foods with uneven thicknesses, like fish fillets and drumsticks. This placement allows the larger, thicker areas to receive more microwave energy in the corners of the dish.

**Position** tender areas of foods like asparagus and broccoli towards center to prevent tender tips from receiving too much microwave energy and overcooking.

**Arrange** foods of uniform size, like stuffed mushrooms, muffins and baking potatoes in a ring. This arrangement allows equal exposure to microwave energy.

**Center** smaller pieces when cooking foods of different size and density, like cut-up chicken parts. This placement helps all pieces to cook evenly.

**Placement on oven tray** should allow microwaves to reach all sides of the food, whether you are cooking several items like baked apples or one item like a meatloaf. When placement alone is not enough, the recipe will direct you to stir, turn over, rearrange or turn the dish.

# Food Handling Techniques

In addition to food placement, other techniques help to promote even cooking. The terms below appear frequently in the recipes in this book. Understanding how and why these techniques are performed will help you get the best results from microwave recipes.

**Cover** foods during cooking to retain heat and moisture and to speed cooking. Cover selection is discussed on page 7. Carefully remove any covering away from you to avoid contact with hot steam.

**Stir** foods to equalize food temperature and shorten cooking time. Stirring is usually done midway through the cooking period and should be done from the outside to center of dish.

**Turn** refers to rotating the dish rather than moving the food itself. Turning the dish promotes even heating for foods which cannot be stirred or rearranged.

**Turn over** means repositioning the food itself so that the upper and lower surfaces are reversed. This can be done to individual pieces like salmon steaks, or to an entire food, like a whole cauliflower.

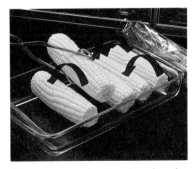

**Rearrange** refers to changing the position of foods within the dish. Since food on the outside receives more energy than food in the center, rearrange center pieces to outside, and outside pieces to center.

**Shield** means to cover sensitive areas with foil to prevent overcooking. Use small amounts of foil to cover areas of a dish or parts of food which cook too quickly. Foil must be at least 1 inch from oven walls.

**Standing time** allows microwaved foods to finish cooking by heat conduction after they are removed from the oven. Dense foods like roasts, whole poultry and large whole vegetables usually call for longer standing times.

# Browning Meats, Poultry and Fish

Some types and cuts of meat brown naturally when cooked. Others brown only because of conventional cooking methods, like broiling or frying. Because of high fat content and longer cooking time, larger cuts of meat and large whole poultry will brown in the microwave. Smaller pieces cook so quickly in the microwave that they do not have time to brown. To give microwaved meats a browned appearance, use browning agents, coatings or microwave browning utensils.

## Browning Techniques

**Browning agents** include sauces, glazes, oils, crumb mixtures and dry seasoning or coating mixes. Some are applied before microwaving; others are added during or after. They can enhance the color and flavor of meats, poultry and fish.

**Brush** meats with liquid browning agents before microwaving. Some can be applied full strength; others should be diluted with an equal amount of water or melted butter. Try bouquet sauce and melted butter, or for distinctive flavor as well as color try Worcestershire, steak, soy, teriyaki or barbecue sauce.

**Rub** poultry with liquid browning agents after drying surface thoroughly and before microwaving. Use Worcestershire sauce or diluted bouquet sauce. Or try soy or teriyaki sauce for an Oriental flavor.

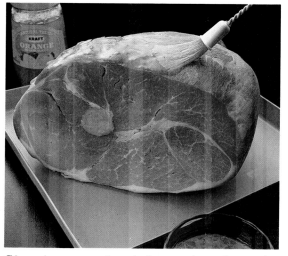

**Glaze** ham or poultry during or after microwaving. Brush or spread preserves, jelly or other glaze mixtures over the surface. Try orange marmalade on poultry or ham, and mint jelly on lamb.

12

Pictured left to right: conventionally cooked meat, microwaved meat, microwave-treated meat

**Sprinkle or pat** dry mixtures on meat, poultry or fish for added color, flavor and texture. Try packaged coating products, seasoning mixes (like dry soup mixes), herbs and spices, bouillon granules, butter-crumb combinations, crushed potato chips, French-fried onion rings or Parmesan cheese mixtures.

**Browning utensils** will brown meats and sandwiches much the same way a conventional skillet does. These utensils have a special coating on the bottom which absorbs microwave energy to reach a temperature high enough for browning. Preheat the dish as directed by the manufacturer, then brown foods on both sides.

# Microwave Defrosting

Your microwave oven can really save you time when defrosting frozen foods. Microwave defrosting is much faster than defrosting in the refrigerator, and prevents the growth of bacteria that may occur when defrosting foods at room temperature. Defrosting meat just before cooking helps reduce moisture loss.

## Defrosting Techniques

**Unwrap** food and place in a dish or on a roasting rack. A wax paper cover will hold warmth around the food and help it defrost more quickly and evenly.

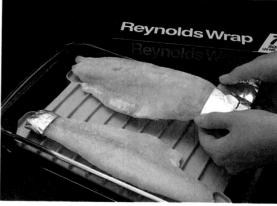

**Shield** smaller, thinner areas of food with small amounts of foil to prevent them from beginning to cook. If cooking begins during defrosting, those portions will change color and feel warm.

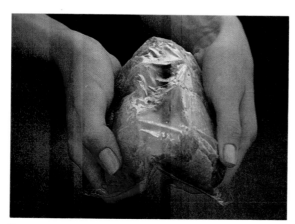

**Rearrange**, break up, turn over or stir to promote even distribution of heat. Whenever possible, remove food that is defrosted, then continue to defrost the remainder. Items in pouches can be moved about by flexing the package.

**Standing time** may be necessary to complete defrosting at the end of the defrost time. The standing time allows internal heat to reach parts of the food not completely defrosted. Large, dense foods or delicate foods are most likely to require standing time after defrosting.

# Microwave Reheating

Foods reheated in your microwave retain their freshly-cooked flavor and texture. Microwave reheating makes leftovers taste better and allows you to prepare foods in advance to be heated at serving time. Busy family members who eat at different times can reheat their portion of an entire meal right on the serving plate.

## Reheating Techniques

**Food on plates** should be arranged with thick, dense parts to the outside and smaller, thinner parts to the inside. Foods should be the same temperature. Cover filled plates and turn once during heating.

**Layered casseroles** which cannot be stirred should be heated at power level 7. To heat evenly, turn dish several times.

**Sweet rolls** should be placed on paper towels or napkins to absorb moisture. Use paper towels to line a plate or basket when heating several rolls. Be careful not to overheat.

**Casseroles** should be stirred at least once during reheating to distribute heat evenly. Always cover main dishes when reheating. If they have been refrigerated, reheat at power level 8.

**Bread loaves and sandwiches** should be wrapped in paper towels or napkins before reheating. The paper covering absorbs moisture so bread surfaces remain dry. Bread products toughen if overheated, so watch carefully.

**Test for doneness** by carefully touching the bottom of the plate after heating. If it feels warm from contact with the heated food, the food is ready to serve.

# Microwaving Convenience Foods

Convenience foods are great when you're in a hurry, and microwave heating gets them on the table even faster. Many products have microwave instructions on the package, and these should be followed carefully for best results. Use your microwave to defrost frozen desserts and coffee cakes for unexpected guests. When you don't feel like cooking, microwave prepared entrées or frozen dinners for a quick and easy meal. Use the following tips and chart as guidelines.

## Defrosting Cream Pies, Cakes and Brownies

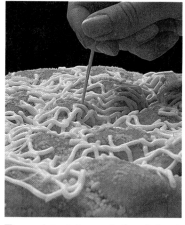

**Remove** cream pie from foil pan and place in pie plate or glass dish. Microwave as directed in chart, opposite. Pie is defrosted when wooden pick can be easily inserted. Let stand for 5 minutes.

**Remove** cake or brownies from foil pan. Place on paper towel-lined plate. Microwave at ③ as directed in chart, opposite. A higher power may melt the topping or frosting.

**Turn** plate 2 times during defrosting. If frosting begins to soften, remove food from oven and let stand to complete defrosting. When a wooden pick can be easily inserted, defrosting is completed.

## Microwaving TV Dinners

**Remove** metal tray from box and discard foil cover. (If food is covered with plastic, follow microwave instructions on carton.) Remove bread and cake-like items from tray; set aside.

**Cover** entire tray with wax paper to retain heat and reduce spattering. Place tray in center of oven. Microwave for half the time as directed in chart, opposite.

**Turn over** main course food items and stir vegetable and pasta mixtures. Microwave remaining time. Dessert may be microwaved in a custard cup for 20 to 30 seconds.

## Convenience Foods Chart

### DEFROSTING

| ITEM | MICROWAVE TIME | POWER LEVEL | PROCEDURE |
|---|---|---|---|
| **Coffee cake,** 6½ to 15 oz. | 1 to 4 min. | 3 | Follow photo directions, opposite. Let stand for 5 minutes. |
| **Pound cake,** 9½ to 12⅞ oz. 16 oz. | ¾ to 1½ min. 1 to 2 min. | 3 3 | Follow photo directions, opposite. Let stand for 5 minutes. |
| **Cheese cake,** 10 oz. 17 to 19 oz. | 1 to 3½ min. 1½ to 4 min. | 3 3 | Follow photo directions, opposite. Let stand for 10 to 15 minutes. |
| **Frosted layer cake,** 10 to 13¾ oz. 15¾ to 18 oz. 21 to 24 oz. | 1 to 3½ min. 1½ to 4 min. 3½ to 6 min. | 3 3 3 | Follow photo directions, opposite. Two- and three-layer cakes can be defrosted on Styrofoam® base or serving plate. Let stand for 15 to 20 minutes. |
| **Brownies,** 13 oz. | 1 to 3 min. | 3 | Follow photo directions, opposite. Let stand for 5 minutes. |
| **Cream pie,** 14 oz. | ¾ to 2 min. | 3 | Follow photo directions, opposite. Let stand for 5 minutes. |

### MICROWAVING

| ITEM | TOTAL TIME | POWER LEVEL | PROCEDURE |
|---|---|---|---|
| **TV dinner,** 2-compartment trays 12 to 13¼ oz. | 6 to 7 min. | High | Follow photo directions, opposite. |
| 3-compartment trays 8¾ to 16 oz. | 6 to 12 min. | High | Follow photo directions, opposite. |
| 4-compartment trays 10¼ to 22 oz. | 7 to 12 min. | High | Follow photo directions, opposite. |
| **Frozen main dish entrée,** 6¼ to 9½ oz. | 3½ to 7 min. | High | Remove packaging. Place food in baking dish or casserole and cover with wax paper or microwave in paperboard tray. Microwave as directed until heated. Stir food or turn dish after half the time. |
| 10 to 13 oz. | 6 to 9 min. | High 3 min., then 5 | |
| 14 to 21 oz. | 5 to 15 min. | High 5 min., then 5 | |

# Microwave Melting, Softening and Warming

Melting, softening and warming foods in the microwave is faster and easier since constant watching or stirring is not necessary. Microwaves heat from all sides instead of from the bottom only, so you don't have to worry about scorching and burning. Microwave directly in the measuring, mixing or serving container to save clean-up time.

## Melting Techniques

**Chocolate** can be melted in a custard cup or small bowl. Microwave one to three squares at ⑦ for 3½ to 4 minutes; five squares for 4½ to 5 minutes. Melt just until soft.

**Butter** can be melted in a measure or small bowl. Microwave 1 to 4 tablespoons at HIGH for 45 seconds to 1¼ minutes; ¼ to ½ cup for 1¼ to 1¾ minutes.

**Jams and jellies** can be spooned into a bowl and melted for toppings. Microwave at HIGH for 30 to 60 seconds until melted.

## Softening Techniques

**Cream cheese** can be softened in a serving dish or bowl. Remove foil wrap. Microwave 3 oz. at HIGH for 25 seconds; 8 oz. for 45 seconds, just until softened.

**Ice cream**, often too firm to serve easily, can be softened for easy scooping. Remove any foil from carton. Microwave at ⑤ for 15 to 30 seconds per pint.

## Warming Techniques

**Ice cream toppings** can be heated in a bowl or in the jar, if less than half full, with metal lid removed. Microwave at HIGH for 1 to 1¼ minutes. Stir before serving.

**Baby food** should be transferred to a custard cup or serving dish. Microwave a 3½- to 4¾-oz. jar at HIGH for 15 to 30 seconds. Stir and check temperature before serving.

**Baby bottles** of glass or dishwashersafe plastic can be warmed with top removed. Microwave 4 ounces (room temperature) at HIGH for 20 seconds. If refrigerated, add 10 to 20 seconds. Test on inner wrist.

# Using the Microwave With Other Appliances

Some foods turn out better when you combine microwave cooking with conventional cooking. Use the microwave to get a head start on poultry and large cuts of meat, then finish on the charcoal grill. Make toast and waffles conventionally while you heat fillings and toppings in the microwave. As you learn its special capabilities, it will be easy to use the microwave in combination with other appliances.

## Fillings, Sauces and Toppings

**Toast** bread conventionally for sandwiches. Use the microwave to heat fillings, sauces or toppings. Watch carefully; dough and cheese will toughen with overheating.

**Waffles** made with a waffle iron can be topped with syrup, preserves or canned pie filling warmed in the microwave. Heat topping in serving bowl until warm.

**Sauces** for cakes, such as angel food, or crêpes prepared conventionally, can be microwaved without danger of scorching. Heat sauce in serving bowl until warm.

## Meats and Poultry

**Pork chops** and other meats can be browned on top of the range in a glass ceramic casserole and then microwaved in the same dish to complete the cooking. Cooking is fast and clean-up is easy.

**Whole chickens** and pieces, Cornish game hens and small turkeys can be partially cooked in the microwave. Then transfer to the charcoal grill for barbecued flavor and color.

**Spare ribs** and other slow-cooking meats are done faster using the microwave first and then the grill. Begin with partial cooking in the microwave and then transfer to the grill for browning and that special barbecued flavor.

# Converting Conventional Recipes to Microwave

Converting some conventional recipes to microwave cooking can be as easy as reducing the cooking time and adding less moisture; others may need additional changes. Choose recipes for foods which microwave well, following the guidelines below. When in doubt, look for a microwave recipe in this book which is similar to the recipe you are converting.

## Conversion Guidelines

**Naturally moist foods**, like vegetables, fruits, poultry and seafood, microwave well. You may not need as much liquid as the conventional recipe indicates.

**Foods cooked in a sauce**, like casseroles and other main dishes, generally adapt well to microwaving. Choose conventional recipes that indicate covered cooking, steaming or simmering.

**Rich foods** are good microwave candidates because of their high fat and/or sugar content. Examples are candies, moist cakes, dessert fondues and bar cookies.

**Do not convert** recipes for foods which require deep-fat frying or a dry, crusty surface. Conventional recipes for yeast breads may need specially formulated microwave instructions.

**Select recipes** that call for ingredients and methods that adapt well to the microwave. Begin with the same amount of the main solid ingredient and determine further steps by comparing the conventional recipe to a similar one for the microwave.

**Reduce liquid** to about three-fourths of the amount called for in the conventional recipe. You can always add more moisture if needed, but usually this is unnecessary because of the microwave's moist cooking process.

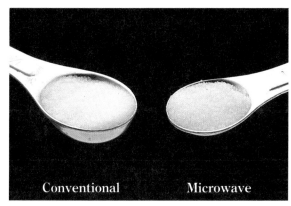

**Less seasoning** is usually needed, especially salt and highly flavored herbs and spices like garlic and cayenne. Small amounts of mild seasonings do not need to be changed. Adjust seasonings after microwaving.

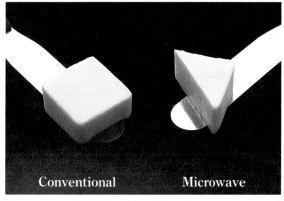

**Compare added fat** since fat attracts energy and affects the cooking time. Small amounts of butter or oil can be used for flavoring but are not necessary to prevent sticking.

**Follow microwave instructions** regarding dish size, placement, covering, rearranging and power level. Some techniques will be common to both conventional and microwave cooking; determine others, such as standing time, by checking a similar microwave recipe.

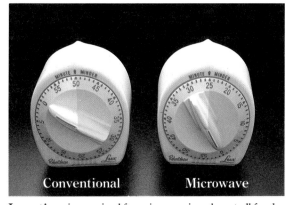

**Less time** is required for microwaving almost all foods. Again, use a microwave recipe as a guide or reduce conventional time by one-third to one-half, checking food after minimum time to avoid overcooking.

# Microwave Meal Planning

The microwave oven's speed and versatility are big helps in menu planning.
Sometimes you may want to use the microwave to prepare the entire meal. Other times you
will want to cook only one item, or just reheat foods before serving. To avoid last-minute rushing, plan
your meal-preparation schedule to take advantage of standing and holding times. The
following techniques and sample menus will show you how.

## Planning Techniques

**Early in the day**, prepare foods which do not need to be hot when served. These include cakes served at room temperature, chilled puddings and gelatin salads, and poultry for sandwich fillings or salads.

**Foods which reheat easily** can be prepared hours before mealtime. Reheat just before serving. Early preparation and reheating simplifies meal preparation and often enhances the flavor. Examples are spaghetti sauce, soup and stew.

**Standing time** is the time needed to complete cooking after microwaving. Use the standing time required for large, dense items like roasts to microwave foods with shorter heating times, like appetizers and breads.

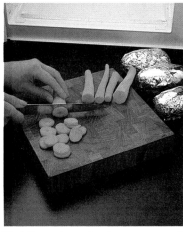

**Holding time** is the amount of time certain foods will retain their heat after cooking is completed. Wrapping large, dense foods like potatoes in foil after microwaving will increase holding time.

**Last-minute heating** and preparation is reserved for foods which heat quickly, like dinner rolls, or cool quickly, like some vegetables.

# Brunch Menu

## Time Management

### Day Before
Prepare pastry shell. Cool, cover and set aside.

### Early on Day of Brunch
Prepare fruit juice of your choice. Cover and refrigerate.

Combine compote ingredients. Cover and refrigerate in serving dish.

Microwave and crumble bacon.

Prepare brunch cake as directed.

### Thirty Minutes Before Serving
Prepare quiche egg mixture; microwave as directed.

### Five Minutes Before Serving
Cut brunch cake into serving pieces.

# Lunch Menu

*Bratwurst in Buns*
page 47

*German Potato Salad*
page 95

*Relish Tray*

*Carrot Cake*
page 105

## Time Management

*Early on Day of Lunch*

Prepare carrot cake as directed. Cover and refrigerate.

Prepare relish tray. Cover and refrigerate.

*Twenty Minutes Before Serving*

Prepare German potato salad as directed. Cover and set aside.

Microwave bratwurst as directed. Place in buns.

# Dinner Menu

Glazed Ham
page 60

Acorn Squash
page 93

Broccoli au Gratin
page 94

Tangy Lemon Pie
page 102

## Time Management

### Day Before

Prepare graham cracker crust, page 108. Cool, cover and set aside.

### Early on Day of Dinner

Prepare pie filling. Pour into prepared crust and refrigerate.

### One Hour Fifteen Minutes Before Serving

Microwave broccoli; drain and set aside. Prepare cheese sauce; refrigerate.

Prepare glaze for ham. Prepare and microwave ham.

### Twenty Minutes Before Serving

Tent ham with foil for standing time.

Microwave squash; remove from oven and wrap with foil to retain heat during standing time.

Reheat cheese sauce at ⑦ for about 2 minutes, until hot, stirring occasionally. Add broccoli. Continue as directed in recipe.

Carve ham.

Mash squash, if desired.

# Recipes

# Appetizers

Appetizers add a festive touch to your dinner menu or cocktail party. Microwaving lets you heat appetizers right on the serving tray, so they go from the microwave oven to the table in minutes. Replenishing and reheating for late comers is easier, too.

## Meatballs in Sauce

**Code: M-1 Well, C-5 Medium**
TOTAL COOKING TIME: 19 minutes
Makes 24 to 30 meatballs

MEATBALLS:
- **1 lb. ground beef**
- **⅓ cup finely chopped onion**
- **1 egg, beaten**
- **⅓ cup dry unseasoned bread crumbs**
- **¼ teaspoon salt**
- **⅛ teaspoon pepper**

POLYNESIAN SAUCE:
- **1 can (10½ oz.) condensed tomato soup**
- **1 can (8 oz.) pineapple chunks, drained**
- **¼ cup packed brown sugar**
- **¼ teaspoon salt**

CREAMY MUSTARD SAUCE:
- **1 can (10½ oz.) condensed cream of celery soup**
- **1 cup dairy sour cream**
- **2 tablespoons prepared mustard**

Mix all meatball ingredients. Form into 1-in. balls. Place in 12 × 8-in. baking dish. Microwave at ⑦ for 7 to 9 minutes, or until firm and no longer pink, stirring once to rearrange. Drain.

In 1½-qt. casserole mix all ingredients for one of the desired sauces. Stir in cooked meatballs. Microwave at ⑦ for 8 to 10 minutes, or until hot, stirring 2 times.

### Cocktail Sausages in Sauce
Follow the recipe above, substituting 3 pkgs. (5 oz. each) cocktail sausages for cooked meatballs.

Pictured clockwise: Rumaki, Meatballs in Creamy Mustard Sauce, Meatballs in Polynesian Sauce

## Rumaki

TOTAL COOKING TIME: 9 minutes
Makes 18 appetizers

- **6 slices bacon**
- **1 can (8 oz.) whole water chestnuts, drained**
- **½ cup teriyaki sauce**

Cut bacon slices into thirds. Wrap one piece of bacon around each water chestnut. Secure with wooden pick. Place in 9-in. pie plate. Pour teriyaki sauce over appetizers. Let stand for at least 30 minutes. Drain. Place on roasting rack. Microwave at HIGH for 8 to 9 minutes, or until bacon is cooked.

### Chicken Liver Rumaki
Follow the recipe above, substituting ½ lb. chicken livers for water chestnuts. Microwave as directed, or until chicken livers are cooked.

## Hot Mexican Dip

**Code: C-5 Medium**
TOTAL COOKING TIME: 6 minutes
Makes about 4 cups

- **1 can (16 oz.) refried beans**
- **1 jar (8 oz.) pasteurized process cheese spread**
- **1 can (4 oz.) chopped green chilies**
- **Dash chili powder**
- **Corn chips**

In 1-qt. casserole mix all ingredients except corn chips. Microwave at ⑥ for 5 to 6 minutes, or until cheese melts, stirring once. Serve with corn chips.

### Taco Dip
Follow the recipe above, omitting cheese spread and chili powder. Mix in 1 cup taco sauce. Green chilies can be omitted, if desired. Decrease microwave time to 3½ to 4½ minutes.

# Stuffed Mushrooms ↓

Manual: Warm +
TOTAL COOKING TIME: 4½ minutes
Serves 6 to 8

**8 oz. fresh mushrooms**
**1 tablespoon butter or margarine**
**2 tablespoons chopped green onion**
**2 tablespoons dry unseasoned bread crumbs**
**2 tablespoons dairy sour cream**
 **Dash salt**
 **Dash pepper**

## Walnut-Stuffed Mushrooms

Follow the recipe at left, adding ⅓ cup chopped walnuts and a dash of dried thyme leaves with the chopped stems.

## Cheese-Stuffed Mushrooms

Follow the recipe at left, substituting 2 tablespoons shredded Cheddar cheese for the sour cream.

Follow photo directions for microwaving, below.

## *How to Microwave Stuffed Mushrooms*

**Remove** stems from mushrooms. Set caps aside; finely chop stems. In 1-qt. casserole or small bowl combine chopped stems, butter and green onion. Microwave at HIGH for 1 to 1½ minutes, or until stems are tender.

**Stir** in remaining ingredients except mushroom caps. Spoon filling into mushrooms caps. Place on plate. Microwave at HIGH for 2 to 3 minutes, or until hot, turning plate once.

# Crab Canapés ↓

Manual: Warm +
TOTAL COOKING TIME: 2 minutes
Makes 20 canapés

- 1 can (6½ oz.) crab meat, rinsed and drained
- ½ cup mayonnaise or salad dressing
- ¼ cup shredded Cheddar cheese
- 2 tablespoons chopped green onion
- 1 teaspoon prepared horseradish
- 1 teaspoon catsup
- ½ teaspoon Worcestershire sauce
- 20 Melba rounds

In small bowl mix all ingredients except Melba rounds. Spread evenly on Melba rounds. Place on paper towel-lined plate. Microwave at 7 for 1½ to 2 minutes, or until cheese melts, rotating plate once.

## Shrimp Canapés
Follow the recipe above, substituting 1 can (4½ oz.) shrimp, drained, for crab meat.

## Salmon Canapés
Follow the recipe above, substituting 1 can (6½ oz.) salmon, drained, cleaned and flaked, and ½ teaspoon dried dillweed for crab meat, horseradish and Worcestershire sauce.

# Beef Taco Chips

Code: M-1 Well    Manual: Medium
TOTAL COOKING TIME: 4½ minutes
Serves 3 to 4

- ¼ lb. ground beef
- ¼ cup finely chopped onion
- ½ teaspoon chili powder
- ¼ teaspoon salt
- ⅛ teaspoon cumin
  Dash garlic powder
- ½ cup shredded Monterey Jack cheese
- 12 to 15 taco chips
  Taco sauce, optional

Crumble beef into 1-qt. casserole. Add onion, chili powder, salt, cumin and garlic powder. Microwave at HIGH for 1½ to 2½ minutes, or until beef is no longer pink, stirring once.

Arrange chips on 10-in. paper plate or paper towel-lined plate. Spoon meat mixture onto chips. Top with cheese. Microwave at 7 for 1½ to 2 minutes, or until cheese melts, turning plate 1 or 2 times. Serve with taco sauce.

# Beverages

Hot beverages, from an everyday cup of coffee to a special holiday punch, are an easy way to warm yourself or your guests. You can microwave beverages right in the serving mug or drinking cup. The fresh flavor is retained even when reheating.

## Irish Coffee ↑

Manual: Medium
TOTAL COOKING TIME: 2 minutes
Serves 1

¾ cup strong black coffee
3 tablespoons Irish whiskey
    Sweetened whipped cream

Pour coffee into 8-oz. mug or cup. Microwave at HIGH for 1 to 2 minutes, or until very hot. Stir in whiskey. Top with whipped cream.

### Spiced Coffee

Follow the recipe above, substituting 1 tablespoon milk, 1 to 2 teaspoons sugar and dash ground nutmeg for the whiskey. Add a stick of cinnamon and top with whipped cream.

## Hot Mulled Cider ↑

Code: B-1 Medium
TOTAL COOKING TIME: 11 minutes
Makes about 4 cups

1 qt. apple cider
4 cinnamon sticks
1 tablespoon whole allspice
6 whole cloves
1 tablespoon honey
1 orange, sliced

In large bowl or 2-qt. measure combine all ingredients. Microwave at HIGH for 10 to 11 minutes, or until mixture boils. Stir. Strain into mugs. Garnish with additional orange slices and cinnamon sticks, if desired.

## Apple Nog ↑

Code: B-2 Warm
TOTAL COOKING TIME: 11 minutes
Makes about 4 cups

2 eggs, beaten
¼ cup sugar
1 teaspoon ground cinnamon
   Dash ground nutmeg
3 cups milk
1 cup apple juice

In medium bowl or 2-qt. measure blend all ingredients. Microwave at 7 for 10 to 11 minutes, or until very hot but not scalded, stirring 1 or 2 times. Serve with cinnamon sticks and whipped cream, if desired.

## Instant Cocoa

Manual: Warm +
TOTAL COOKING TIME: 1½ minutes
Serves 1

1 envelope (1 oz.) instant hot cocoa mix
¾ cup hot water

Place contents of envelope in 8-oz. mug or cup. Stir in hot water. Microwave at HIGH for 1 to 1½ minutes, or until hot. Stir before serving. Top with marshmallows or whipped topping, if desired.

## Chateau Spiced Burgundy ↑

Code: B-1 Hot
TOTAL COOKING TIME: 9 minutes
Makes about 6 cups

1 cup sugar
2 cups water
1 orange, sliced
8 whole cloves
2 sticks cinnamon
1 qt. Burgundy wine

In medium bowl combine sugar, water, orange slices, cloves and cinnamon sticks. Microwave at HIGH for 8 to 9 minutes, or until boiling. Strain into punch bowl. Stir in wine. Garnish with additional orange slices and cinnamon sticks, if desired.

## Instant Coffee

Manual: Warm +
TOTAL COOKING TIME: 1½ minutes
Serves 1

1 teaspoon instant coffee
¾ cup hot water

Place instant coffee in 8-oz. mug or cup. Stir in hot water. Microwave at HIGH for 1 to 1½ minutes, or until hot. Stir before serving.

# Soups & Stews

Soups and stews can be simmered in the microwave at any time of year without heating up your kitchen. Microwave simmering also helps retain ingredient nutrition, texture and color. Heat a single serving in a soup bowl or serve a crowd right from the cooking tureen or casserole.

## How to Microwave Water-Base Soups

Code: S-2 Medium

**Place** soup bones or poultry carcass and hot water in large casserole. Microwave, covered, at HIGH for at least 1 hour. Remove meat; cut into small pieces.

**Return** meat to broth; discard bones. Add remaining ingredients as indicated in recipe. Microwave, covered, at HIGH until vegetables are tender.

## How to Microwave Cream Soups

Code: S-5 Medium

**Melt** butter in casserole at HIGH. Blend in flour, salt and pepper. Blend in half of the cream or milk. Stir in meat, fish or vegetables as indicated in recipe.

**Microwave** at 7 until thickened, stirring 1 or 2 times. Blend in remaining cream or milk. Microwave at 7 until hot, stirring once.

## How to Microwave Dried Bean, Split Pea or Lentil Soups

Code: S-4 Medium

**Presoak** dried beans with hot water in large casserole by microwaving, covered, at HIGH until boiling. Boil for 2 minutes. Let stand for 1 hour. Do not drain. (Do not presoak split peas or lentils.)

**Add** remaining ingredients as indicated in recipe to soaked dried beans, or combine split peas or lentils with water and remaining ingredients in large casserole.

**Microwave**, covered, at HIGH until tender, stirring 2 or 3 times. For thicker soup lightly mash beans, peas or lentils.

Pictured: Split Pea Soup, page 36

35

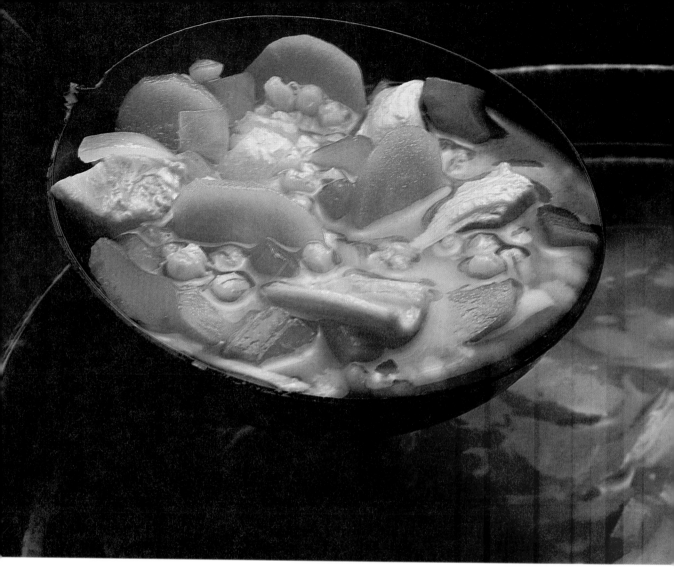

## Turkey Soup With Barley ↑

Code: S-2 Medium
TOTAL COOKING TIME: 2 hours 15 minutes
Serves 6 to 8

 1 turkey carcass
12 cups hot water
½ cup pearl barley
 1 cup chopped onion
 1 cup chopped celery
 1 cup thinly sliced carrots
 1 teaspoon salt
¼ teaspoon pepper

Cut turkey carcass to fit 5-qt. casserole. Place in casserole with hot water; cover. Microwave at HIGH for 1 hour. Remove carcass. Remove meat from bones. Discard bones and skin. Add meat, barley, onion, celery, carrots, salt and pepper to water. Re-cover. Microwave at HIGH for 1 to 1¼ hours, or until barley is tender.

NOTE: HEAT & HOLD method can be used, page 4.

## Split Pea Soup

Code: S-4 Medium
TOTAL COOKING TIME: 45 minutes
Serves 4 to 6

 1 lb. dried green split peas, rinsed
¼ cup thinly sliced celery
 1 medium carrot, thinly sliced
 1 small onion, chopped
¼ lb. salt pork, scored
 1 teaspoon salt
¼ teaspoon pepper
¼ teaspoon dried thyme leaves, optional
 6 to 8 cups hot water

In 3-qt. casserole combine peas, celery, carrot, onion, salt pork, salt, pepper, thyme and 6 cups hot water. Cover. Microwave at HIGH for 40 to 45 minutes, or until peas are tender, stirring 2 or 3 times. For thinner soup, add hot water as needed.

# Onion Soup →

Code: V-3 Hot   Manual: Hot

TOTAL COOKING TIME: 35½ minutes
Serves 4

- 6  tablespoons butter or margarine
- 2  extra-large or 4 large onions, halved
    and thinly sliced (about 1½ lbs.)
- 2  cans (10½ oz. each) condensed
    beef consommé
- 1  cup hot water
- ¼  cup dry white wine
- 1  tablespoon Worcestershire sauce
- ⅛  teaspoon pepper
- 8  slices French bread, ½-in. thick
- ½  cup shredded Swiss cheese, divided
- 1  tablespoon plus 1 teaspoon grated
    Parmesan cheese, divided

In 3-qt. casserole place butter and onions; cover. Micro-wave at HIGH for 18 to 20 minutes, or until tender, stirring 2 times. Add consommé, hot water, wine, Wor-cestershire sauce and pepper. Re-cover. Microwave at HIGH for 8 to 9 minutes, or until boiling.

Divide among four individual 15-oz. casseroles or soup bowls. Top each casserole with two slices French bread. Sprinkle 2 tablespoons Swiss cheese and 1 teaspoon Parmesan cheese over bread in each casserole. Arrange in circle in oven and microwave at ⑦ for 5½ to 6½ minutes, or until cheese melts.

# Cream of Mushroom Soup

Code: S-5 Medium   Manual: Warm +

TOTAL COOKING TIME: 9¼ minutes
Serves 4 to 6

- 2  tablespoons butter or margarine
- 3  tablespoons all-purpose flour
- ½  teaspoon salt
- ¼  teaspoon white pepper
- 1  teaspoon instant chicken bouillon
    granules
- 2  tablespoons finely chopped onion
- 2  cups half and half, divided
- 2  cups chopped fresh mushrooms

In 2-qt. casserole melt butter at HIGH for 1 to 1¼ minutes. Stir in flour, salt, white pepper, bouillon gran-ules and onion. Blend in 1 cup half and half. Add mushrooms. Microwave at ⑦ for 6 minutes to thicken, stirring 1 or 2 times. Blend in remaining half and half. Microwave at ⑦ for 1 to 2 minutes, or until hot.

## Corn Chowder

Follow the recipe above, substituting 1 can (16 oz.) whole kernel corn, drained, for mushrooms.

## Shrimp Crab Bisque ↑

Code: S-5 Warm    Manual: Warm +
TOTAL COOKING TIME: 9¼ minutes
Serves 4 to 6

  2  tablespoons butter or margarine
  2  tablespoons all-purpose flour
  ½  teaspoon salt
  ¼  teaspoon white pepper
  1  teaspoon instant chicken bouillon granules
  2  tablespoons finely chopped onion
     Dash red pepper sauce
1½  cups half and half, divided
  ½  lb. raw medium shrimp, shelled and
     deveined
  1  can (6 oz.) crab meat, rinsed and drained
  ½  cup white wine

In 2-qt. casserole microwave butter at HIGH for 1 to 1¼ minutes, or until butter melts. Stir in flour, salt, white pepper, bouillon granules, onion and red pepper sauce. Blend in 1 cup half and half. Add shrimp and crab meat. Microwave at ⑦ for 6 minutes to thicken, stirring 1 or 2 times. Blend in remaining half and half and wine. Microwave at ⑦ for 1 to 2 minutes, or until hot. Garnish with chopped chives, if desired.

## Beef Stew (pictured opposite)

Code: S-3 Medium
TOTAL COOKING TIME: 1 hour 40 minutes
Serves 6 to 8

1½  lbs. beef stew meat, cut into
     ¾- to 1-in. cubes
  ⅓  cup all-purpose flour
  1  teaspoon salt
  ½  teaspoon dried marjoram leaves
  ⅛  to ¼ teaspoon pepper
  2  teaspoons instant beef bouillon granules
2½  cups hot water
1½  cups thinly sliced carrots
  2  medium onions, cut into eighths
  2  medium potatoes, cut into ¾-in. pieces

Follow photo directions for microwaving, opposite.

### Pork Stew

Follow the recipe above, substituting pork for beef. Substitute dried thyme leaves for marjoram. Substitute chicken bouillon for beef bouillon.

### Lamb Stew

Follow the recipe above, substituting lamb for beef. Substitute dried rosemary leaves for marjoram.

NOTE: HEAT & HOLD method can be used, page 4.

## How to Microwave Beef Stew

**Combine** beef, flour, salt, marjoram and pepper in 3-qt. casserole. Stir to coat. Dissolve bouillon granules in hot water; add to meat. Cover. Microwave at HIGH for 10 minutes. Stir. Reduce power to ③.

**Microwave** for 30 minutes. Stir in vegetables. Re-cover. Microwave at ③ for 45 to 60 minutes, or until meat and vegetables are tender, stirring 2 times.

39

# Sauces & Gravies

Sauces turn everyday foods into elegant ones, bringing new flavors to vegetables, eggs, seafood, meats and poultry. They microwave evenly without danger of scorching. Gravies capture the flavor of meat drippings, and heat in the microwave without the constant stirring needed on the range top.

## Sauce & Gravy Chart

| MICROWAVING | | | | |
|---|---|---|---|---|
| Follow photo directions, opposite. | | | | |
| **BROWN GRAVY** | **FAT FROM MEAT DRIPPINGS** | **FLOUR** | **JUICES FROM MEAT DRIPPINGS PLUS WATER** | **MICROWAVE TIME** |
| **1 cup, thin** | 1 tbsp. | 1 tbsp. | 1 cup | 3 to 4 min. |
| **1 cup, medium** | 2 tbsp. | 2 tbsp. | 1 cup | 4 to 5 min. |
| **1 cup, thick** | 3 tbsp. | 3 tbsp. | 1 cup | 5 to 6 min. |
| **2 cups, thin** | 2 tbsp. | 2 tbsp. | 2 cups | 6 to 7 min. |
| **2 cups, medium** | 4 tbsp. | 4 tbsp. | 2 cups | 8 to 9 min. |
| **2 cups, thick** | 6 tbsp. | 6 tbsp. | 2 cups | 11 to 12 min. |
| **WHITE SAUCE** | **BUTTER** | **FLOUR** | **MILK** | **MICROWAVE TIME AT HIGH: BUTTER** | **MICROWAVE TIME AT 7: SAUCE** |
| **1 cup, thin** | 1 tbsp. | 1 tbsp. | 1 cup | 1 min. | 4 to 5 min. |
| **1 cup, medium** | 2 tbsp. | 2 tbsp. | 1 cup | 1¼ min. | 5 to 6 min. |
| **1 cup, thick** | 3 tbsp. | 3 tbsp. | 1 cup | 1¼ min. | 7 to 8 min. |
| **2 cups, thin** | 2 tbsp. | 2 tbsp. | 2 cups | 1¼ min. | 9 to 10 min. |
| **2 cups, medium** | 4 tbsp. | 4 tbsp. | 2 cups | 1¼ min. | 10 to 11 min. |
| **2 cups, thick** | 6 tbsp. | 6 tbsp. | 2 cups | 1¼ min. | 11 to 12 min. |

## How to Microwave Gravy

**Measure** fat into 1-qt. or 1½-qt. casserole as directed in chart, opposite. Blend in flour.

**Stir** in liquid until smooth. Microwave at HIGH as directed, or until thickened, stirring 1 or 2 times.

## How to Microwave White Sauce

**Place** butter in 1-qt. or 1½-qt. casserole as directed in chart, opposite. Microwave at HIGH as directed, or until butter melts. Blend in flour.

**Stir** in milk. Microwave at 7 as directed, or until thickened, stirring 1 or 2 times. Season to taste.

**Cheddar Cheese Sauce.** Stir ½ to 1 cup shredded Cheddar cheese into 1 cup White Sauce, above, until melted. Serve sauce over vegetables or eggs.

**Swiss Cheese Sauce.** Stir ½ to 1 cup shredded Swiss cheese into 1 cup White Sauce, above, until melted. Serve over seafood, veal, vegetables or eggs.

**Herb Sauce.** For each cup of White Sauce, above, add ¼ to ½ teaspoon dried herb leaves to butter before melting. Continue as directed, above.

# Meats

Meat is the main attraction of many meals, and an important source of protein. The microwave cooks meat quickly and helps retain the natural juices lost in conventional cooking. Defrosting and reheating are other bonuses your microwave brings to cooking and serving meats.

## How to Defrost Large, Thick Roasts

**Remove** packaging. Place roast on roasting rack. Microwave for half the time as directed in chart, page 46. Turn roast over.

**Shield** warm areas with foil. Microwave remaining time, turning roast over 1 or 2 times. Let stand for 20 to 30 minutes, or until wooden skewer inserted to center meets little resistance.

## How to Defrost Chops, Steaks and Flat Roasts

**Remove** packaging. Arrange meat on roasting rack. Microwave for half the time as directed in chart, page 46. Turn meat over and rearrange.

**Shield** warm areas on large steaks and flat roasts with foil. Microwave remaining time, or until meat is pliable. Let stand for 5 to 10 minutes.

## How to Defrost Ground Meat

**Remove** packaging. Place meat in casserole. Microwave for two-thirds the time as directed in chart, page 46, scraping off and removing soft pieces 2 or 3 times.

**Break** up remaining meat before last one-third of time. Microwave remaining time, or until meat is softened but still cold. Let stand for 5 minutes (1 pound) to 10 minutes (over 1 pound).

Pictured clockwise: Standing rib roast, page 46, hamburger, page 46, Saucy Pork Chops, page 59, Shish Kabobs, page 62

# Microwave "Roasting"

Your microwave oven saves time when cooking beef, pork and lamb roasts, and the results are tender and juicy. Follow the steps below and check the chart on page 46 for specific timings. Remember that microwaved foods continue cooking during standing times, so remove the roast when the internal temperature reaches the degree indicated in chart.

## How to Roast Meat in a Microwave

**Insert** temperature probe or microwave thermometer into roast so tip is in the center of meatiest portion, not touching bone or fat. (See Owner's Guide.)

**Place** roast, fat side down, on roasting rack. Microwave for half the time as directed in chart, page 46. Turn roast over.

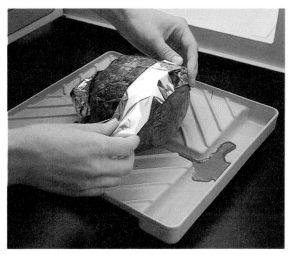

**Shield** edges, thin areas and areas which appear to be cooking more quickly. Microwave remaining time. Turn pork roasts 2 or 3 times during cooking.

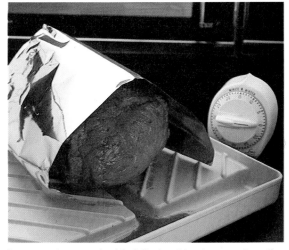

**Let** stand, tented with foil, for 10 minutes. Standing time allows the roast to complete cooking and makes carving easier.

# Microwave "Braising"

Braising, or cooking meat in liquid, is an ideal cooking method for pot roasts and other less tender cuts of meat. Microwave braising is similar to conventional braising, but less liquid is needed because there is little evaporation. To retain as much steam and moisture as possible, microwave meat in a casserole with a tight-fitting lid or in a cooking bag. Meat will continue cooking and tenderizing during the standing time.

## How to Braise Roasts in a Microwave

Code: S-1 Medium

**Pierce** roast deeply and thoroughly with long-tined fork to tenderize before microwaving. If desired, marinate roast in refrigerator for several hours or overnight.

**Place** roast in casserole or cooking bag. Add liquid. Cover or seal. Microwave for half the time as directed in chart, page 46. Turn roast over. Add vegetables, if desired. Re-cover or re-seal.

**Microwave** remaining time, or until tender. Let stand, covered, for 10 minutes to complete cooking and aid in tenderizing.

## Meat Chart

| DEFROSTING | | |
|---|---|---|
| NOTE: See page 4 for Auto Defrost instructions. | | |
| **ITEM** | **MICROWAVE TIME AT 4** | **PROCEDURE** |
| **Beef** | | |
| **Roast,** bone-in and boneless | 5½ to 6½ min./lb. | Follow photo directions, page 43. |
| **Tenderloin** | 3½ to 4½ min./lb. | Remove packaging. Arrange meat on roasting rack. Microwave for half the time. Turn meat over. Shield warm areas with foil. Microwave remaining time, or until pliable. Let stand for 5 to 10 minutes. |
| **Flat roast, Large and small steak** | 4 to 5 min./lb. | Follow photo directions, page 43. |
| **Ribs** | 3 to 6 min./lb. | Follow photo directions, page 43. Let stand for 10 to 15 minutes. |
| **Liver** | 5 to 7 min./lb. | Remove packaging. Place liver on roasting rack. Microwave for one-third the time. Separate and turn over. Microwave remaining time, rearranging 1 or 2 times. Let stand for 5 to 10 minutes. |
| **Stew meat** | 3½ to 5½ min./lb. | Remove packaging. Place meat in baking dish. Microwave for half the time. Break apart; rearrange. Microwave remaining time. Let stand for 5 to 10 minutes. |
| **Ground beef patties,** 1 patty | 2½ to 3½ min. | Remove packaging. Arrange patties on roasting rack. Microwave for half the time. Turn patties over and rearrange. Microwave remaining time. Let stand for 5 to 10 minutes. |
| 2 patties | 3 to 4 min. | |
| **Ground beef** | 4 to 5 min./lb. | Follow photo directions, page 43. |
| **Pork** | | |
| **Roast,** bone-in and boneless | 6 to 8 min./lb. | Follow photo directions, page 43. |
| **Tenderloin** | 5 to 7 min./lb. | Remove packaging. Arrange meat on roasting rack. Microwave for half the time. Turn meat over. Shield warm areas with foil. Microwave remaining time, or until pliable. Let stand for 5 to 10 minutes. |
| **Chops, Ribs** | 3 to 6 min./lb. | Follow photo directions, page 43. Let ribs stand for 10 to 15 minutes. |
| **Stew meat** | 3½ to 5½ min./lb. | Remove packaging. Place meat in baking dish. Microwave for half the time. Break apart; rearrange. Microwave remaining time. Let stand for 5 to 10 minutes. |
| **Ground pork** | 3 to 5 min./lb. | Follow photo directions, page 43. |
| **Lamb** | | |
| **Roasts** | 5 to 8 min./lb. | Follow photo directions, page 43. |
| **Chops** | 4 to 7 min./lb. | Follow photo directions, page 43. |
| **Stew meat** | 4½ to 6½ min./lb. | Remove packaging. Place meat in baking dish. Microwave for half the time. Break apart and rearrange. Microwave remaining time. Let stand for 5 to 10 minutes. |
| **Ground lamb** | 4 to 5 min./lb. | Follow photo directions, page 43. |

| MICROWAVING | | | | |
|---|---|---|---|---|
| Estimate total cooking time. Microwave at High as directed in chart. Reduce power. Continue to microwave for remaining time. | | | | |
| **ITEM** | **TOTAL TIME** | **INTERNAL TEMP.** | **POWER LEVEL** | **PROCEDURE** |
| **Beef Roast,** | | | | |
| bone-in and boneless, less than 4 lbs. | Rare: 9 to 12 min./lb. Med: 10½ to 13½ min./lb. Well: 12 to 14½ min./lb. | 120° 130° 150° | High 5 min., then 5 | Follow photo directions, page 44. |
| greater than 4 lbs. | Same as above. | | High 8 min., then 5 | |

| ITEM | TOTAL TIME | INTERNAL TEMP. | POWER LEVEL | PROCEDURE |
|---|---|---|---|---|
| **Tenderloin,** | | | | |
| less than 2 lbs. | Rare: 7½ to 9½ min./lb. | 120° | High 3 min., then 5 | Shield ends and 1 inch down sides. Place on roasting rack. Microwave, turning roast over once and removing shield after two-thirds time. Let stand for 10 minutes, tented with foil. |
| | Med: 8 to 10 min./lb. | 130° | | |
| | Well: 9½ to 11½ min./lb. | 150° | | |
| greater than 2 lbs. | Same as above. | | High 5 min., then 5 | |
| **Pot roast** | 40 to 50 min./lb. | | High 10 min., then 5 | Follow photo directions, page 45. |
| **Patties,** ¼ inch thick | | | | Place patties on roasting rack. Microwave, turning over once. To use browning dish, preheat according to directions. Reduce time. Let stand for 1 to 2 minutes. |
| 1 patty | 2½ to 3 min. | | High | |
| 2 patties | 3 to 3½ min. | | High | |
| 4 patties | 4½ to 5 min. | | High | |
| **Pork** | | | | |
| **Boneless roast\*** | 12 to 16 min./lb. | 170° | High 5 min., then 5 | Follow photo directions, page 44. |
| **Tenderloin** | 12½ to 16½ min./lb. | 170° | High 3 min., then 5 | Shield ends and 1 inch down sides. Place tenderloin on roasting rack. Microwave, turning roast over once and removing shield after two-thirds the time. Let stand for 10 to 15 minutes, tented with foil. |
| **Pork chops** | 16½ to 18½ min./lb. | | High 3 min., then 5 | Place on roasting rack or in baking dish. Microwave, turning and rearranging 1 or 2 times. Let stand for 3 to 5 minutes. |
| **Ham,** rolled (boneless), fully cooked | 10 to 15 min./lb. | 130° | High 5 min., then 5 | Follow photo directions for microwave roasting, page 44. |
| **Lamb** | | | | |
| **Leg of lamb,** bone-in | Med: 9 to 12¾ min./lb. | 130° | High 5 min., then 5 | Follow photo directions, page 44. |
| | Well: 10 to 14 min./lb. | 150° | | |
| **Boneless roast,** shoulder or leg | Med: 10½ to 14½ min./lb. | 130° | High 5 min., then 5 | Follow photo directions, page 44. |
| | Well: 12 to 15½ min./lb. | 150° | | |
| **Bacon and Sausages** | | | | |
| **Bacon,** | | | | Place slices on paper towel or roasting rack. Microwave, turning rack 1 or 2 times. Let stand for 3 to 5 minutes. |
| 1 slice | 1 to 1½ min. | | High | |
| 2 slices | 2 to 2½ min. | | High | |
| 4 slices | 3 to 5 min. | | High | |
| 8 slices | 6 to 8½ min. | | High | |
| **Bratwurst,** fully cooked | | | | Place bratwurst on plate. Microwave, turning over and rearranging once. |
| 1 | ¾ to 1¼ min. | | High | |
| 2 | 1¼ to 1¾ min. | | High | |
| 4 | 2 to 3 min. | | High | |
| **Hot dogs,** fully cooked | | | | Place hot dogs on plate. Microwave, turning over and rearranging once. |
| 1 | ½ to ¾ min. | | High | |
| 2 | ¾ to 1¼ min. | | High | |
| 4 | 1¾ to 2¾ min. | | High | |
| **Sausage links,** precooked | | | | Place links on roasting rack. Microwave, turning over and rearranging once. |
| 2 | 1½ to 2 min. | | High | |
| 4 | 1½ to 1¾ min. | | High | |
| uncooked | | | | Place links on roasting rack. Microwave, turning over and rearranging once. |
| 2 | 2 to 3½ min. | | High | |
| 4 | 2½ to 4 min. | | High | |

*Bone-in roast not recommended for microwaving.

# Beef

## ← Basic Pot Roast

**Code: S-1 Medium**
TOTAL COOKING TIME: 2 hours 55 minutes
Serves 4 to 6

- 3 to 3½-lb. beef chuck roast
- 1 envelope (1¼ oz.) onion soup mix
- 1 can (10¾ oz.) condensed beef broth
- 3 medium potatoes, cut into eighths
- 1½ cups thinly sliced carrots

Pierce roast on both sides with fork. Place in cooking bag. Pour onion soup mix and beef broth over roast. Close bag with strip cut from cooking bag or with string. Place bag in 12 × 8-in. baking dish. Microwave at HIGH for 10 minutes. Turn dish. Reduce power to ③; microwave for 1 hour. Turn roast over. Add potatoes and carrots to cooking bag. Reseal. Microwave at ③ for 1½ to 1¾ hours, or until meat and vegetables are tender.

## Italian Pot Roast

**Code: S-1 Medium**
TOTAL COOKING TIME: 2 hours 10 minutes
Serves 4 to 6

- 3 to 3½-lb. beef chuck roast
- 1 can (16 oz.) whole tomatoes
- 1 can (6 oz.) tomato paste
- ¾ teaspoon Italian seasoning
- ¼ teaspoon sugar

Pierce roast on both sides with fork. Place in cooking bag. Mix tomatoes, tomato paste, Italian seasoning and sugar. Pour over roast in bag. Close bag with strip cut from cooking bag or with string. Place bag in 12 × 8-in. baking dish.

Microwave at HIGH for 10 minutes. Turn dish. Reduce power to ③; microwave for 1 hour. Turn bag over. Microwave at ③ for 45 to 60 minutes, or until roast is fork tender. Let stand for 10 minutes.

48

## Corned Beef ⌃

Code: S-1 Medium
TOTAL COOKING TIME: 1 hour 55 minutes
Serves 6 to 8

2½ to 3-lb. corned beef brisket with
     seasoning packet
1 cup hot water

Place corned beef in 3-qt. casserole with contents of
seasoning packet and water. Cover. Microwave at
HIGH for 10 minutes. Turn beef over. Reduce power to
3. Microwave for 1½ to 1¾ hours, or until tender,
turning over after half the time. Let stand, covered, for
10 minutes. To serve, carve diagonally across the grain
into thin slices.

### Corned Beef With Cabbage

Follow the recipe above. Remove beef; cover. Cut one
large head cabbage into eight wedges. Place in cooking
juices; cover. Microwave at HIGH for 10 to 12 minutes,
or until fork tender. Serve with corned beef.

NOTE: HEAT & HOLD method can be used, page 4.
Cover completely with water before microwaving.

## Mexican Shredded Beef

Code: S-1 Medium
TOTAL COOKING TIME: 2 hours 2 minutes
Serves 6 to 8

2½ to 3-lb. fresh beef brisket
1 can (8 oz.) tomato sauce
1 pkg. (1¼ oz.) taco seasoning mix
¾ cup water
    Taco shells or flour tortillas

Prepare beef brisket as directed for Corned Beef, left.
Remove from cooking liquid and discard liquid. Cut beef
into shreds. Return to 3-qt. casserole. Stir in tomato
sauce, taco seasoning mix and water. Cover. Microwave at HIGH for 5 to 7 minutes, or until hot, stirring
once. Use in tacos, burritos or enchiladas.

# Beef Brisket With Horseradish

Code: S-1 Medium, S-5 Medium
TOTAL COOKING TIME: 2 hours 9 minutes
Serves 6 to 8

2½ to 3-lb. fresh beef brisket
1 small onion, sliced
2 teaspoons instant beef bouillon granules
1 bay leaf

HORSERADISH SAUCE:
 ¼ cup chopped onion
 2 tablespoons butter or margarine
 1 tablespoon plus 1½ teaspoons
     all-purpose flour
 ¼ cup plus 2 tablespoons prepared
     cream-style horseradish
 2 tablespoons sugar
 2 tablespoons cider vinegar
 2 whole cloves
 1 cup reserved cooking liquid from meat

Prepare beef brisket as directed for Corned Beef, page 49, adding onion, bouillon granules and bay leaf to water. Discard all but 1 cup of strained cooking liquid.

In 4-cup measure place chopped onion and butter. Microwave at HIGH for 3 to 4 minutes, or until onion is tender, stirring once. Blend in flour. Stir in reserved cooking liquid and remaining sauce ingredients. Microwave at HIGH for 4 to 5 minutes, or until thickened, stirring once. Remove cloves before serving.

# Bacon Steak

Code: S-1 Medium
TOTAL COOKING TIME: 1 hour 40½ minutes
Serves 4 to 6

 4 slices bacon, cut up
1½ lbs. beef boneless round steak, ½-in. thick
 ⅓ cup all-purpose flour
 ½ teaspoon salt
 ¼ teaspoon pepper
 1 onion, sliced and separated into rings
 2 teaspoons instant beef bouillon granules
1½ cups hot water

Place bacon in 12 × 8-in. baking dish. Microwave at HIGH for 4½ to 5½ minutes, or until crisp. Remove from dish. Trim fat from steak. Pound to ¼-in. thickness. Cut into serving-size pieces. Combine flour, salt and pepper in large plastic food storage bag. Shake steak in flour mixture to coat. Add steak and remaining flour mixture to bacon drippings. Top with onion and bacon.

Dissolve bouillon granules in hot water. Pour over steak. Cover with plastic wrap. Microwave at HIGH for 5 minutes. Turn dish. Reduce power to ③. Microwave for 45 minutes. Turn steak over; re-cover. Microwave at ③ for 30 to 45 minutes, or until tender. Let stand for 10 minutes. Skim fat before serving.

# Swiss Steak →

Code: S-1 Medium
TOTAL COOKING TIME: 1 hour 35 minutes
Serves 4 to 6

1½ lbs. beef boneless round steak,
     ½-in. thick
 ⅓ cup all-purpose flour
 ½ teaspoon salt
 ¼ teaspoon pepper
 1 onion, sliced and separated into rings
 1 can (15 oz.) tomato sauce
 ¼ teaspoon sugar

Trim fat from steak. Pound steak to ¼-in. thickness. Cut into serving-size pieces. Combine flour, salt and pepper in large plastic food storage bag. Shake steak in flour mixture to coat.

Place steak and remaining flour mixture in 12 × 8-in. baking dish. Top with onion. Mix tomato sauce and sugar; pour over steak. Cover with plastic wrap. Microwave at HIGH for 5 minutes. Turn dish. Reduce power to ③; microwave for 45 minutes. Turn steak over; re-cover. Microwave at ③ for 30 to 45 minutes, or until tender. Let stand for 10 minutes. Stir sauce.

## Onion Steak

Follow the recipe above, omitting onion, tomato sauce and sugar. Combine 1 can (10¾ oz.) condensed cream of onion soup, 1 tablespoon Worcestershire sauce, 1 teaspoon instant beef bouillon granules and ⅓ cup hot water. Pour over steak. Continue as directed.

# Beef Short Ribs With Wine Sauce

Code: S-1 Medium
TOTAL COOKING TIME: 2 hours 10 minutes
Serves 3 to 4

3 lbs. beef short ribs
1 can (10¾ oz.) condensed golden
     mushroom soup
¾ cup red wine
1 jar (4½ oz.) button mushrooms, drained
⅓ cup cold water
3 tablespoons all-purpose flour

Place ribs in 3- to 5-qt. casserole. Mix soup and wine. Pour over ribs; cover. Microwave at HIGH for 10 minutes. Turn ribs over. Reduce power to ③. Re-cover and microwave at ③ for 45 minutes. Turn ribs over. Add mushrooms. Re-cover and microwave at ③ for 50 to 60 minutes, or until ribs are fork tender. Let stand, covered, for 10 minutes. Remove ribs with slotted spoon to serving platter; cover.

Blend cold water and flour. Stir into cooking liquid. Microwave at HIGH for 4 to 5 minutes, or until thickened, stirring once. Skim fat. Pour sauce over ribs.

NOTE: HEAT & HOLD method can be used, page 4.

## How to Microwave Less-Tender Steak

**Trim** fat from steak. Pound steak to ¼-in. thickness. Cut into serving-size pieces. Combine flour and seasonings in large plastic food storage bag.

**Add** steak, shaking to coat. Place steak and remaining flour mixture in baking dish. Add liquid or sauce ingredients. Cover with plastic wrap.

**Microwave** at ③ until tender, turning over after half the time. Let stand for 10 minutes.

## ← Saucy Beef With Chinese Vegetables

Code: M-1 Medium, C-1 Medium
TOTAL COOKING TIME: 19 minutes
Serves 4

  1  lb. beef flank steak
  1  small onion, thinly sliced
  1  tablespoon teriyaki sauce
  1  can (14 oz.) Chinese vegetables, drained
  1  can (10¾ oz.) condensed cream of
       mushroom soup
  ⅛  teaspoon pepper
     Hot cooked rice

Cut steak diagonally across grain into thin slices. Cut slices into 3-in. lengths. Place beef, onion and teriyaki sauce in 2-qt. casserole. Microwave at 7 for 6 minutes, stirring once. Stir in vegetables, soup and pepper. Microwave at 7 for 9 to 13 minutes, or until beef is no longer pink, stirring 2 times. Serve over rice.

## Gingered Beef and Vegetables

Code: C-1 Medium   Manual: Hot
TOTAL COOKING TIME: 23 minutes
Serves 4 to 6

  2  tablespoons cornstarch
  2  tablespoons soy sauce
  ¼  teaspoon ground ginger
  ⅛  teaspoon garlic powder
  1  can (10½ oz.) condensed beef consommé
  1  small onion, thinly sliced
  1  stalk celery, cut into ¼-in. slices
  1  lb. beef boneless sirloin steak, cut across
       the grain into thin strips
  1  pkg. (6 oz.) frozen Chinese pea pods
  8  oz. fresh bean sprouts
  1  cup sliced fresh mushrooms
     Hot cooked rice

In 4-cup glass measure or 1-qt. casserole mix cornstarch, soy sauce, ginger and garlic powder. Slowly blend in consommé. Microwave at HIGH for 4 minutes to thicken, stirring once. Set aside.

In 3-qt. casserole place onion and celery. Cover. Microwave at HIGH for 3 minutes, or until tender-crisp. Stir in beef and sauce. Add frozen pea pods. Microwave at 7 for 8 minutes, stirring to break apart pea pods after half the time. Stir in bean sprouts and mushrooms. Microwave at 7 for 4 to 8 minutes, or until beef is no longer pink, stirring once. Serve over rice.

# Beef Stroganoff

Code: M-1 Rare, C-1 Medium
TOTAL COOKING TIME: 15 minutes
Serves 4 to 6

- 1½ lbs. beef boneless sirloin steak
- 1 teaspoon Worcestershire sauce
- ¼ cup all-purpose flour
- ¼ cup cold water
- 2 teaspoons instant beef bouillon granules
- ¾ cup hot water
- 1 jar (4½ oz.) button mushrooms, drained
- ¼ teaspoon salt
- ⅛ teaspoon pepper
- ¾ cup dairy sour cream
- 1 tablespoon catsup, optional
  Hot cooked noodles

Trim fat from steak; discard. Slice steak across grain into thin strips. Place beef and Worcestershire sauce in 2-qt. casserole. Microwave at 7 for 3 minutes, stirring once. Blend flour and cold water. Stir into beef. Dissolve bouillon granules in hot water; add to beef. Stir in mushrooms, salt and pepper. Microwave at 7 for 10 to 12 minutes, or until beef is no longer pink, stirring 2 or 3 times. Blend in sour cream and catsup. Serve over noodles.

# Meat Loaf ↑

Code: M-2 Medium
TOTAL COOKING TIME: 21 minutes
Serves 4 to 6

- ¾ lb. lean ground beef
- ¼ lb. ground pork
- ¾ cup fresh bread crumbs (about 1 slice)
- 1 can (8 oz.) tomato sauce
- 1 egg
- 1 teaspoon Worcestershire sauce
- ½ teaspoon salt
- ½ teaspoon dried savory leaves, optional

TOPPING:
- ¼ cup catsup
- 2 tablespoons Worcestershire sauce

Mix all ingredients except topping. Press into 9 × 5-in. loaf dish. Microwave at 8 for 10 minutes. Turn dish. Blend catsup and 2 tablespoons Worcestershire sauce. Spread over meat loaf. Microwave at 8 for 9 to 11 minutes, or until internal temperature reaches 150°F. Let stand for 5 minutes.

# Chili

Code: M-1 Well, S-4 Medium
TOTAL COOKING TIME: 30½ minutes
Serves 6 to 8

  1 lb. lean ground beef
  1 medium onion, chopped
  1 small green pepper, chopped
  1 can (16 oz.) whole tomatoes
  1 can (15 oz.) chili beans, drained
  1 can (8 oz.) tomato sauce
  1 can (4 oz.) diced green chilies
  1 medium tomato, chopped, optional
  1 medium carrot, grated, optional
  1 to 2 teaspoons chili powder
  ¼ teaspoon cumin
  ⅛ teaspoon garlic powder

In 3-qt. casserole crumble beef; add onion and green pepper. Cover. Microwave at HIGH for 4½ to 5½ minutes, or until beef is no longer pink. Stir to break up beef. Stir in remaining ingredients. Microwave, uncovered, at 6 for 25 minutes to blend flavors, stirring once.

# Enchilada Casserole

Code: M-1 Well, C-1 Medium
TOTAL COOKING TIME: 16 minutes
Serves 4

  1 lb. lean ground beef
  2 tablespoons chopped onion
  3 cups corn chips
  1½ cups shredded Cheddar cheese, divided
  1 can (8 oz.) whole tomatoes, cut up
  1 can (4 oz.) diced green chilies
  1 teaspoon chili powder
    Shredded lettuce
    Tomato slices

Crumble beef into 2-qt. casserole; add onion. Cover. Microwave at HIGH for 4½ to 5 minutes, or until beef is no longer pink. Drain. Stir in corn chips, 1 cup Cheddar cheese, tomatoes, green chilies and chili powder. Microwave at 8 for 7 to 8 minutes, or until hot. Sprinkle remaining cheese on top. Microwave at 8 for 2 to 3 minutes, or until cheese melts. Garnish each serving with shredded lettuce and tomato slices.

# Lasagna

Code: C-2 Medium
TOTAL COOKING TIME: 46 minutes
Serves 6 to 8

  1 pkg. (8 oz.) uncooked lasagna noodles
  1 lb. lean ground beef
  ½ cup chopped onion
  1 jar (32 oz.) spaghetti sauce
  1 jar (4 oz.) sliced mushrooms, drained
  1 container (16 oz.) ricotta cheese
  1 egg, slightly beaten
  1½ cups shredded mozzarella cheese

Prepare noodles as directed, page 83. Set aside. In 2-qt. casserole crumble beef; add onion. Cover. Microwave at HIGH for 4 to 5 minutes, or until beef is no longer pink. Drain. Stir in spaghetti sauce and mushrooms. In small bowl mix ricotta cheese and egg.

In 12 × 8-in. baking dish layer one-third of the noodles, one-third of the sauce and one-half of the ricotta cheese mixture. Repeat layers twice, omitting ricotta cheese from third layer. Microwave at 8 for 15 to 18 minutes, or until hot, turning dish after half the time. Sprinkle with mozzarella cheese. Microwave at 8 for 6 to 7 minutes, or until cheese melts. Let stand, covered with foil, for 10 minutes.

# Spaghetti Sauce

TOTAL COOKING TIME: 28½ minutes
Serves 4 to 6

  ½ lb. lean ground beef
  ½ cup chopped onion
  ½ cup finely chopped green pepper
  1 clove garlic, minced
  2 cans (15 oz. each) tomato sauce
  1 can (12 oz.) tomato paste
  ¼ cup red wine vinegar
  2 tablespoons packed brown sugar
  1 tablespoon Italian seasoning
  ½ teaspoon salt
  ⅛ teaspoon pepper

In 2-qt. casserole crumble beef; add onion, green pepper and garlic. Cover. Microwave at HIGH for 3 to 3½ minutes, or until beef is no longer pink. Stir in remaining ingredients. Microwave at 6 for 25 minutes to blend flavors, stirring once.

## Cabbage Rolls →

Code: C-2 Medium
TOTAL COOKING TIME: 22 minutes
Serves 4

8  large cabbage leaves
½  cup water
1  lb. lean ground beef
1  cup cooked rice
¼  cup chopped onion
1  egg
1  teaspoon salt
¼  teaspoon pepper
1  can (10¾ oz.) condensed tomato soup,
     divided
1  can (8 oz.) sauerkraut, drained, optional

Follow photo directions for microwaving, below.

### *How to Microwave Cabbage Rolls*

**Place** cabbage and water in large bowl. Cover with plastic wrap. Microwave at HIGH for 5 minutes to soften.

**Mix** beef, rice, onion, egg, salt and pepper with 2 tablespoons soup. Divide among cabbage leaves.

**Fold** in sides. Roll up and secure with wooden picks. Place cabbage rolls, seam sides down, in 12 × 8-in. baking dish.

**Mix** remaining soup and sauerkraut; pour over cabbage rolls. Cover baking dish loosely with plastic wrap. Microwave at HIGH for 12 to 17 minutes, or until heated through, turning dish once.

# Pork

## Country-Style Ribs

**Code: M-8 Medium**
TOTAL COOKING TIME: 1 hour 12 minutes
Serves 4

½ cup chopped onion
1 can (8 oz.) tomato sauce
3 tablespoons packed brown sugar
2 tablespoons lemon juice
1 teaspoon prepared mustard
¼ teaspoon liquid smoke
3 lbs. pork country-style ribs
¾ cup hot water

Follow photo directions for microwaving, below.

### How to Microwave Country-Style Ribs

**Place** onion in 1-qt. casserole. Microwave at HIGH for 2 minutes. Mix in tomato sauce, brown sugar, lemon juice, mustard and liquid smoke. Set aside.

**Combine** ribs and water in 3-qt. casserole. Cover. Microwave at ⑤ for 45 to 55 minutes, or until tender, rearranging once. Drain. Pour sauce over ribs. Microwave, uncovered, for 10 to 15 minutes, or until sauce appears dry.

## Breaded Pork Chops

**Code: M-7 Medium**
TOTAL COOKING TIME: 14 minutes
Serves 4

4 pork chops, ½-in. thick
1 egg, beaten
⅔ cup dry seasoned bread crumbs

Dip each chop in beaten egg, then coat in bread crumbs. Arrange on roasting rack. Microwave at HIGH for 3 minutes. Rearrange. Reduce power to ⑤. Microwave for 8½ to 11 minutes, or until pork near bone is no longer pink, rearranging chops after half the time.

## Stuffed Pork Chops

**Code: M-7 Medium**
TOTAL COOKING TIME: 21 minutes
Serves 4

2 tablespoons chopped onion
2 tablespoons butter or margarine
¾ cup herb-seasoned stuffing mix
¼ cup apple juice
2 tablespoons raisins
⅛ teaspoon salt
⅛ teaspoon pepper
4 pork chops, 1-in. thick, with pocket
1 egg, beaten
⅔ cup dry seasoned bread crumbs

In 1-qt. casserole combine onion and butter. Cover. Microwave at HIGH for 3 minutes, or until tender. Stir in stuffing mix, apple juice, raisins, salt and pepper until moistened. Loosely spoon about one-fourth of stuffing into each chop. Dip each into beaten egg, then coat with bread crumbs.

Arrange chops on roasting rack. Microwave at HIGH for 3 minutes. Turn over. Reduce power to ⑤. Microwave for 14 to 15 minutes, or until pork near bone is no longer pink and internal temperature reaches 170°F, rearranging chops once. Let stand for 5 minutes.

# ← Barbecued Pork Chops

**Code: M-7 Medium**
TOTAL COOKING TIME: 22 minutes
Serves 4

- 1 tablespoon chopped onion
- 1 tablespoon chopped green pepper
- 1 teaspoon butter or margarine
- 2 tablespoons packed brown sugar
- ½ cup catsup
- 2 tablespoons red wine vinegar
- 1 tablespoon plus 1½ teaspoons Worcestershire sauce
- 4 pork chops, ½-in. thick

Follow photo directions for microwaving, below.

### *How to Microwave Barbecued Pork Chops*

**Combine** onion, green pepper and butter in 2-cup measure. Microwave at HIGH for 3 minutes. Stir in brown sugar, catsup, vinegar and Worcestershire sauce. Microwave at 5 for 5 minutes. Stir sauce.

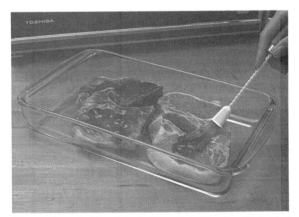

**Place** chops in 12 × 8-in. baking dish. Brush with half of sauce. Microwave at HIGH for 3 minutes. Reduce power to 7. Microwave for 8½ to 11 minutes, or until pork near bone is no longer pink, turning over and brushing with remaining sauce after half the time.

58

## Saucy Pork Chops

Code: M-8 Medium
TOTAL COOKING TIME: 14 minutes
Serves 4

4 pork chops, ½-in. thick
1 envelope (single-serving size) instant
   onion soup mix
1 can (10¾ oz.) condensed cream of
   chicken soup

Place chops in 12 × 8-in. baking dish. Sprinkle with onion soup mix. Top with cream of chicken soup. Microwave at HIGH for 3 minutes. Reduce power to ⑦. Microwave for 8½ to 11 minutes, or until pork near bone is no longer pink, rearranging once. Stir sauce; serve over chops.

## Sweet and Sour Pork

Code: C-1 Medium
TOTAL COOKING TIME: 21 minutes
Serves 4

3 tablespoons cornstarch
¼ cup soy sauce
1 can (8 oz.) pineapple chunks, drained
   and juice reserved
⅓ cup sugar
½ teaspoon salt
½ teaspoon ground ginger
⅛ teaspoon pepper
¼ cup cider vinegar
1 lb. pork boneless loin, cut into 1-in. cubes
1 green pepper, cut into ¼-in. strips
1 can (8 oz.) water chestnuts, drained and
   sliced
2 tablespoons chili sauce
   Hot cooked rice

Blend cornstarch and soy sauce in 2-qt. casserole. Add enough water to pineapple juice to make 1 cup liquid. Stir into cornstarch mixture. Stir in sugar, salt, ginger, pepper and vinegar. Microwave at HIGH for 5 to 6 minutes, or until thickened, stirring once.

Stir in pineapple, pork, green pepper, water chestnuts and chili sauce. Reduce power to ⑦. Microwave for 12 to 15 minutes, or until pork is no longer pink, stirring 2 times. Serve over rice.

## Pork Chili Verde ↑

Code: S-4 Medium
TOTAL COOKING TIME: 57 minutes
Serves 4 to 6

1 medium onion, chopped
1 large clove garlic, minced
1 lb. pork stew meat, ¾-in. cubes
2 tablespoons all-purpose flour
1½ teaspoons salt
⅛ teaspoon pepper
1 can (16 oz.) whole tomatoes
1 can (4 oz.) diced green chilies

In 2-qt. casserole combine onion and garlic. Cover. Microwave at HIGH for 2 minutes. Stir in pork, flour, salt and pepper. Add tomatoes and green chilies. Stir to break up tomatoes. Cover. Microwave at HIGH for 5 minutes. Stir. Reduce power to ⑤. Microwave, covered, for 30 minutes. Stir. Microwave, uncovered, at ⑤ for 15 to 20 minutes, or until pork is tender.

### Beef Chili Verde

Follow the recipe above, substituting beef chuck for pork stew meat.

# Hearty Bavarian Casserole

Code: C-1 Medium
TOTAL COOKING TIME: 23 minutes
Serves 4

- 3 cups coarsely shredded cabbage
- 1 medium apple, chopped
- 1 can (10¾ oz.) condensed cream of onion soup, divided
- ⅓ cup packed brown sugar
- 1 teaspoon caraway seed
- 4 smoked pork chops, ½-in. thick
- 1 lb. fully cooked Polish sausage, cut into 1-in. pieces

In 12 × 8-in. baking dish combine cabbage, apple, half can of soup, brown sugar and caraway seed. Cover with plastic wrap. Microwave at HIGH for 7 to 8 minutes, or until cabbage is tender-crisp, stirring once. Arrange chops and sausage over top. Spoon remaining soup over all. Cover. Microwave at ⑦ for 12 to 15 minutes, or until chops are heated through, rearranging chops after half the time. Let stand for 5 minutes before serving.

# Spring Ham Casserole

Code: C-1 Medium
TOTAL COOKING TIME: 27 minutes
Serves 4 to 6

- 1 pkg. (7 oz.) uncooked spaghetti
- ½ cup chopped celery
- ½ cup chopped onion
- ¼ cup chopped green pepper
- 2 tablespoons butter or margarine
- 2 tablespoons all-purpose flour
- 2 teaspoons instant chicken bouillon granules
- ⅛ teaspoon white pepper
- 1½ cups half and half
- 3 cups cubed fully cooked ham, ½-in. cubes
- 1 jar (4½ oz.) button mushrooms, drained
- ¼ cup grated Parmesan cheese
- 2 tablespoons snipped fresh parsley

Prepare spaghetti as directed, page 83. Set aside. In 2-qt. casserole combine celery, onion, green pepper and butter. Cover. Microwave at HIGH for 3 to 4 minutes, or until onion is tender. Mix in flour, bouillon granules and white pepper. Blend in half and half.

Reduce power to ⑦. Microwave, uncovered, for 4½ to 6 minutes, or until thickened, stirring once. Stir in ham, mushrooms and cooked spaghetti. Microwave at ⑦ for 5 to 7 minutes, or until hot, stirring once. Sprinkle with Parmesan cheese and parsley.

# Glazed Ham →

TOTAL COOKING TIME: 48½ minutes
Serves 6 to 8

- 3 to 3½-lb. fully cooked boneless ham Whole cloves
- 2 cans (8¼ oz. each) sliced pineapple, drained and juice reserved
- 2 tablespoons packed brown sugar
- 1 teaspoon prepared mustard
- ¼ teaspoon ground ginger Maraschino cherries

Score surface of ham into diamonds with diagonal slashes (cut only ¼ inch deep). Stud ham with whole cloves. Place in cooking bag. In 2-cup measure combine pineapple juice, brown sugar, mustard and ginger. Microwave at HIGH for 1 to 1½ minutes, or until sugar dissolves. Stir. Pour over ham. Close bag with strip cut from cooking bag or with string. Place ham in 9 × 9-in. baking dish.

Microwave at HIGH for 5 minutes. Turn over. Microwave at ⑤ for 38 to 42 minutes, or until heated through, turning over after half the time. Let stand for 10 minutes. Arrange ham on serving platter with pineapple slices and cherries. Serve with cooking liquid, if desired.

# Ham Loaf

Code: M-2 Medium
TOTAL COOKING TIME: 21 minutes
Serves 4

- 1¼ lbs. ground fully cooked ham
- ¼ lb. ground pork
- ½ cup soft bread crumbs
- ¼ cup chopped onion
- ¼ cup chopped green pepper
- 2 eggs, slightly beaten
- ¼ cup milk
- ⅓ cup packed brown sugar
- 1 tablespoon prepared mustard
- ⅓ cup pineapple juice

In large bowl mix ham, pork, bread crumbs, onion, green pepper, eggs and milk. Press into 9 × 5-in. loaf dish. Mix brown sugar and mustard; spread over loaf. Pour pineapple juice over all. Microwave at ⑧ for 18 to 21 minutes, or until firm in center, turning dish after half the time. Let stand for 5 minutes.

# Lamb

## Marinated Lamb Roast

Code: M-5 Medium

TOTAL COOKING TIME: 1 hour 11½ minutes
Serves 6 to 8

**4 to 5-lb. leg of lamb, boned, rolled and tied**

MARINADE:
**½ cup olive oil**
**¼ cup dry white wine**
**¼ cup lemon juice**
**2 cloves garlic, minced**
**1 teaspoon salt**
**¼ teaspoon pepper**
**¼ teaspoon dried rosemary leaves**
**¼ teaspoon dried thyme leaves**
**¼ teaspoon dried oregano leaves**

MINT SAUCE:
**1 cup white wine vinegar**
**¼ cup sugar**
**1 tablespoon plus 1 teaspoon dried mint leaves**
    **Dash salt**

Place lamb in plastic bag. Combine marinade ingredients in 2-cup measure. Microwave at HIGH for 1 to 1½ minutes, or until warm. Pour over lamb. Close bag and refrigerate at least 4 hours or overnight.

Before microwaving lamb, combine mint sauce ingredients in 2-cup measure. Microwave at [5] for 5 to 6 minutes, or until boiling. Cool.

Remove lamb from bag. Discard marinade. Place lamb, fat side up, on roasting rack. Microwave at HIGH for 5 minutes. Turn over. Reduce power to [5]. Microwave for 43 to 59 minutes, or until internal temperature reaches 150°F in center, turning over after half the time. Let stand, tented with foil, for 10 to 15 minutes. Serve with mint sauce.

## Shish Kabobs →

Code: M-1 Medium

TOTAL COOKING TIME: 27 minutes
Serves 4

**½ cup mint jelly**
**¼ cup vegetable oil**
**¼ cup wine vinegar**
**1 lb. lamb boneless shoulder, cubed**
**4 wooden skewers, 10-in. long**
**½ green pepper, cut into 8 pieces**
**4 large mushrooms**
**4 cherry tomatoes**
**4 small pearl onions**

In 1-qt. casserole combine jelly, oil and vinegar. Microwave at HIGH for 2 to 2½ minutes, or until heated and jelly melts, stirring after half the time. Add lamb. Cover and refrigerate at least 4 hours.

Thread each skewer, beginning with lamb and repeating lamb between green pepper, mushroom, cherry tomato, green pepper and onion. Place kabobs on roasting rack. Cover with wax paper. Microwave at [7] for 7 to 9 minutes, or until desired doneness, rotating and rearranging after the first 3 minutes and then every 2 minutes. Serve with rice, if desired.

### Pork Kabobs Code: M-1 Well

Follow the recipe above, substituting ½ cup teriyaki sauce and two slices lemon for jelly, oil and vinegar. Substitute 1 lb. pork boneless loin, cubed, for lamb. In 1-qt. casserole combine teriyaki sauce and lemon slices. Microwave at HIGH for 1 to 1½ minutes, or until heated. Add pork. Marinate and assemble as directed. Microwave at [7] for 13 to 14 minutes, or until pork is no longer pink, rotating and rearranging as directed.

### Beef Kabobs Code: M-1 Medium

Follow the recipe above, substituting ⅔ cup Italian dressing for jelly, oil and vinegar. Substitute 1 lb. beef boneless sirloin, cubed, for lamb. Pour dressing into 1½-qt. casserole. Microwave at HIGH for 1 minute to heat. Add beef. Marinate as directed. Place green pepper and onion in 1-qt. casserole. Cover. Microwave at HIGH for 1 to 1½ minutes, or until tender-crisp. Assemble as directed. Microwave at [7] for 5 to 7 minutes, or until desired doneness, rotating and rearranging as directed.

# Lamb Curry

Code: M-1 Well, C-1 Medium

TOTAL COOKING TIME: 20 minutes
Serves 6

1 lb. ground lamb
1 small onion, chopped
⅔ cup chopped green pepper
1 tablespoon curry powder
3 cups cooked rice
⅓ cup half and half
1 medium tomato, chopped
½ teaspoon salt

Crumble lamb into 2-qt. casserole. Microwave at 7 for 4 to 5 minutes, or until lamb is no longer pink, stirring to break apart every 2 minutes. Drain fat. Add onion, green pepper and curry powder. Cover. Microwave at 7 for 4 to 5 minutes, or until vegetables are tender, stirring after half the time. Add rice, half and half, tomato and salt. Cover. Microwave at 7 for 10 minutes to heat. Sprinkle with peanuts before serving, if desired.

# *Poultry*

Poultry is one of the most nutritious and economical foods at your meat counter. Its natural juiciness makes it perfect for microwaving to serve hot or cold. Sauces and browning agents will perk up the color and flavor of microwaved poultry. Try precooking whole poultry or pieces in the microwave and finishing them on the charcoal grill. The microwave oven takes poultry from the freezer to casseroles, salads and sandwiches in no time.

## *How to Defrost Whole Poultry*

**Remove** packaging. Place poultry on roasting rack. Microwave for one-fourth the time as directed in chart, page 67. Turn rack. Microwave for additional one-fourth of the time.

**Turn** bird over. Shield warm areas with foil, if needed. Microwave remaining time, or until pliable, turning rack once. Rinse under cold running water. Let stand as directed in chart.

## *How to Defrost Poultry Pieces*

**Remove** packaging. Place poultry on roasting rack. Microwave for half the time as directed in chart, page 67. Separate pieces. Arrange on rack with meatiest parts to the outside.

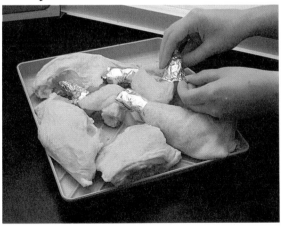

**Shield** warm areas with foil. Microwave remaining time, or until pliable. Let stand for 5 to 10 minutes. Rinse under cold running water.

Pictured: Cornish hens, page 67 and Confetti Rice, page 85

## How to Microwave Whole Poultry

Code: P-3 Medium

 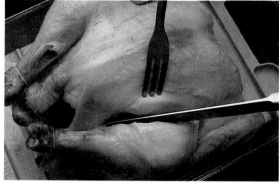

**Wash** and dry poultry well. Rub on browning agent, if desired. Place bird, breast side down, on roasting rack or in baking dish. Microwave for half the time as directed in chart, opposite. Turn rack once.

**Turn** bird breast side up. (Glaze, if desired.) Microwave remaining time, or until inner thigh meat is no longer pink and juices run clear. Let stand as directed.

## How to Microwave Whole Chicken in a Bag

Code: P-3 Well

 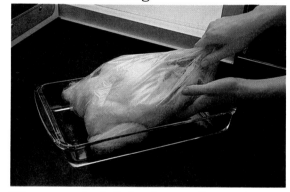

**Place** chicken in cooking bag. Seal with string, rubber band or strip cut from end of bag. Place chicken, breast side down, in baking dish.

**Microwave** for half the time as directed in chart, opposite. Turn chicken breast side up. Microwave remaining time, or until inner thigh meat is no longer pink and juices run clear. Let stand for 5 minutes.

## How to Microwave Poultry Pieces

Code: P-1 Medium

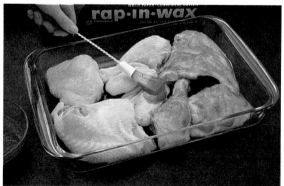 

**Arrange** poultry pieces with meatiest parts to outside of baking dish. If desired, brush with barbecue sauce or rub with browning agent. Cover with wax paper. For steamed poultry, cover with plastic wrap.

**Microwave** for half the time as directed in chart, opposite. Rearrange poultry so that areas which appear less cooked are to outside of dish. Cover and microwave remaining time, or until meat near bone is no longer pink. Let stand for 5 to 10 minutes.

66

## DEFROSTING

NOTE: See page 4 for Auto Defrost instructions.

| ITEM | MICROWAVE TIME AT 4 | PROCEDURE |
|------|---------------------|-----------|
| Whole chicken | 3½ to 5½ min./lb. | Follow photo directions, page 65. Let stand for 5 to 10 minutes. |
| Chicken quarters | 4½ to 5½ min./lb. | Follow photo directions, page 65. |
| Chicken pieces | 3 to 5 min./lb. | Follow photo directions, page 65. |
| Chicken breasts, boneless | 6 to 8 min./lb. | Follow photo directions, page 65. |
| Whole turkey | 3½ to 6 min./lb. | Follow photo directions, page 65. Let stand for 20 to 30 minutes in cool water. |
| Turkey breast | 3 to 6 min./lb. | Follow photo directions, page 65. Let stand for 5 to 10 minutes. |
| Turkey parts | 3½ to 6 min./lb. | Follow photo directions, page 65. |
| Cornish hens | 5 to 7 min./lb. | Follow photo directions, page 65. Let stand for 5 to 10 minutes. |
| Duckling | 4½ to 6 min./lb. | Follow photo directions, page 65. Let stand for 5 to 10 minutes. |

## MICROWAVING

Estimate total cooking time. Microwave at High as directed in chart. Reduce power. Continue to microwave for remaining time as directed.

| ITEM | TOTAL TIME | POWER LEVEL | PROCEDURE |
|------|-----------|-------------|-----------|
| Whole chicken | 6 to 8 min./lb. | High | Follow photo directions, opposite. Let stand, tented with foil, for 5 to 10 minutes. |
| Chicken pieces, boneless or bone-in | 5 to 7 min./lb. | High | Follow photo directions, opposite. |
| Whole turkey | 12 to 15 min./lb. | High 10 min., then 5 | Follow photo directions, opposite. Let stand, tented with foil, for 20 to 30 minutes. |
| Turkey breast | 11 to 15 min./lb. | High 5 min., then 5 | Follow photo directions, opposite. Let stand, tented with foil, for 10 to 20 minutes. |
| Turkey pieces, 2 pieces | 12 to 16 min./lb. | High 3 min., then 5 | Follow photo directions, opposite. |
| 3 or more pieces | 12 to 16 min./lb. | High 5 min., then 5 | Follow photo directions, opposite. |
| Cornish hens | 5½ to 8 min./lb. | High | Follow photo directions, opposite. Let stand, tented with foil, for 5 to 10 minutes. |
| Duckling | 7 to 9 min./lb. | High 10 min., then 5 | Place duckling on roasting rack breast side down. Divide total cooking time in half. Microwave at High for 10 minutes. Drain fat. Reduce power. Microwave remaining first half of time. Drain fat. Turn duckling over. Microwave remaining half of time, turning rack once. Let stand, tented with foil, for 5 to 10 minutes. |

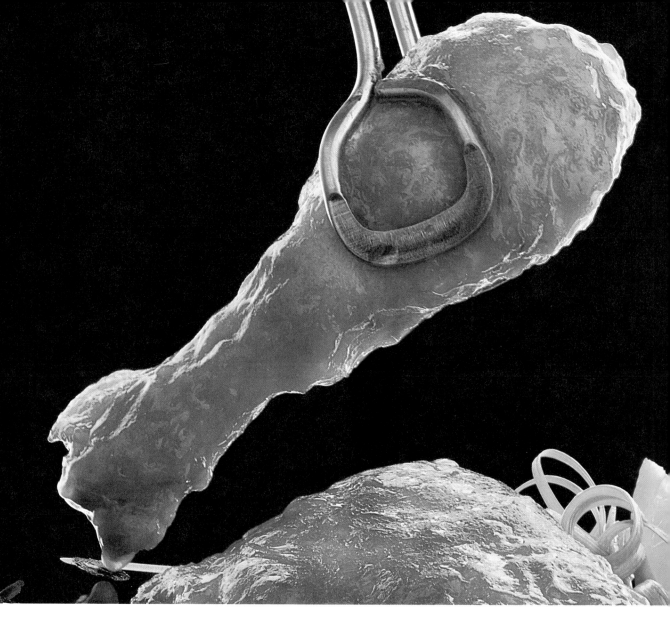

## How to Microwave Chicken With Sauce

**Arrange** 2½ to 3 pounds chicken pieces in 12 × 8-in. baking dish, skin side up, with meatiest portions toward outside of dish. Cover dish with wax paper. Microwave at HIGH for 10 minutes. Turn pieces over. Drain.

**Combine** sauce ingredients; pour over chicken. Cover. Microwave at 7 until chicken near bone is no longer pink, turning pieces over after half the time. Let stand, covered, for 5 minutes.

# Chicken With Orange Sauce

Code: P-2 Medium
TOTAL COOKING TIME: 35 minutes
Serves 4 to 6

**2½ to 3-lb. broiler-fryer chicken, cut up**
**1 cup orange juice**
**½ cup chili sauce**
**1 tablespoon packed brown sugar**
**1 tablespoon soy sauce**
**1 teaspoon prepared mustard**
**1 clove garlic, minced**
**2 tablespoons cornstarch**
**2 tablespoons cold water**

In 12 × 8-in. baking dish arrange chicken pieces, skin side up, with meatiest portions toward outside of dish. Cover with wax paper. Microwave at HIGH for 10 minutes. Drain. Turn pieces over.

Combine orange juice, chili sauce, brown sugar, soy sauce, prepared mustard and garlic; pour over chicken. Cover. Microwave at 7 for 18 to 22 minutes, or until chicken near bone is no longer pink, turning pieces over after half the time. Remove to serving plate; cover.

Blend cornstarch and cold water. Stir into hot cooking liquid. Microwave at HIGH for 2 to 3 minutes, or until thickened. Stir. Serve with chicken.

# Chicken With Mushroom Sauce

Code: P-2 Medium
TOTAL COOKING TIME: 33 minutes
Serves 4 to 6

**2½ to 3-lb. broiler-fryer chicken, cut up**
**1 can (10¾ oz.) condensed golden mushroom soup**
**¼ cup sherry**
**8 oz. fresh mushrooms, sliced**
**½ teaspoon seasoned salt**
**⅛ teaspoon pepper**

Arrange chicken pieces in 12 × 8-in. baking dish, skin side up, with meatiest portions toward outside of dish. Cover with wax paper. Microwave at HIGH for 10 minutes. Turn pieces over. Drain.

Mix soup, sherry, mushrooms, salt and pepper; pour over chicken. Cover. Microwave at 7 for 20 to 23 minutes, or until chicken near bone is no longer pink, turning pieces over after half the time. Let stand, covered, for 5 minutes.

# Easy Curried Chicken

Code: P-2 Medium
TOTAL COOKING TIME: 35 minutes
Serves 4 to 6

**2½ to 3-lb. broiler-fryer chicken, cut up**
**1 can (10¾ oz.) condensed cream of chicken soup**
**1 can (8 oz.) crushed pineapple, drained**
**½ cup raisins**
**1 tablespoon curry powder**

In 12 × 8-in. baking dish arrange chicken pieces, skin side up, with meatiest portions toward outside of dish. Cover with wax paper. Microwave at HIGH for 10 minutes. Turn pieces over. Drain.

Combine soup, pineapple, raisins and curry powder; pour over chicken. Cover. Microwave at 7 for 20 to 25 minutes, or until chicken near bone is no longer pink, turning pieces over after half the time. Let stand, covered, for 5 minutes.

# Chicken Marengo

Code: P-2 Medium
TOTAL COOKING TIME: 33 minutes
Serves 4 to 6

**2½ to 3-lb. broiler-fryer chicken, cut up**
**8 oz. fresh mushrooms, sliced**
**1 pkg. (1½ oz.) spaghetti sauce mix**
**1 can (16 oz.) whole tomatoes**
**¼ cup white wine**

In 12 × 8-in. baking dish arrange chicken pieces, skin side up, with meatiest portions toward outside of dish. Cover with wax paper. Microwave at HIGH for 10 minutes. Drain.

Turn pieces over; top with sliced mushrooms. Combine spaghetti sauce mix, tomatoes and wine, stirring to break up tomatoes. Pour over chicken. Cover. Microwave at 7 for 20 to 23 minutes, or until chicken near bone is no longer pink, turning pieces over after half the time. Let stand, covered, for 5 minutes.

# Chicken With Spanish Rice

TOTAL COOKING TIME: 35 minutes
Serves 4

- 1 cup uncooked long grain rice
- 1 pkg. (1¼ oz.) Spanish rice mix
- ¼ cup finely chopped onion
- ½ teaspoon salt
- 1¾ cups hot water
- 2½ to 3-lb. broiler-fryer chicken, cut up

In 3-qt. casserole combine rice, rice mix, onion, salt and hot water. Top with chicken pieces. Cover. Microwave at HIGH for 10 minutes. Turn pieces over. Cover. Reduce power to ⑥. Microwave for 20 to 25 minutes, or until rice is tender and chicken near bone is no longer pink, turning over after half the time. Let stand for 5 minutes. Stir rice before serving.

# Chicken Fricassee

Code: P-2 Medium
TOTAL COOKING TIME: 49 minutes
Serves 4

- 6 slices bacon
- 2½ to 3-lb. broiler-fryer chicken, cut up
- 2 carrots, cut into 1-in. pieces
- 1½ cups hot water
- 2 teaspoons instant chicken bouillon granules
- 1 tablespoon dried parsley flakes
- 1 teaspoon salt
- ½ cup all-purpose flour
- ½ cup half and half
- 2 egg yolks, slightly beaten

Place bacon between several layers of paper towels. Microwave at HIGH for 6 to 7 minutes, or until crisp. Crumble. Set aside.

Place chicken in 3-qt. casserole. Add carrots. In 2-cup measure combine hot water, bouillon granules, parsley flakes and salt. Pour over chicken and carrots. Add bacon. Cover. Microwave at HIGH for 10 minutes. Turn over. Cover. Reduce power to ⑦. Microwave for 20 to 25 minutes, or until chicken near bone is no longer pink, turning over after half the time. Discard carrots. Remove chicken to serving platter; cover.

Blend flour and half and half. Stir into cooking liquid. Microwave at HIGH for 4 to 5 minutes, or until thickened, stirring 1 or 2 times. Stir a small amount of hot mixture into egg yolks. Return to hot mixture, stirring constantly. Microwave at ⑤ for 1 to 2 minutes, or until thickened, stirring 1 or 2 times. Serve with chicken.

# Creamy Almond Chicken

TOTAL COOKING TIME: 12 minutes
Serves 4

- 4 slices bacon
- 2 whole boneless chicken breasts, halved and skin removed
- 1 can (10¾ oz.) condensed cream of onion soup
- 2 tablespoons sherry
- ½ teaspoon seasoned salt
- ⅛ teaspoon pepper
- ¼ cup sliced almonds

Place bacon in 12 × 8-in. baking dish. Cover with wax paper. Microwave at HIGH for 2 minutes. Wrap bacon slice around each chicken breast lengthwise. Arrange in baking dish with meatiest portions toward outside of dish. Cover dish with wax paper. Microwave at HIGH for 5 minutes.

Combine soup, sherry, seasoned salt and pepper. Pour over chicken. Cover. Microwave at ⑦ for 3 to 5 minutes, or until chicken is no longer pink. Let stand for 5 minutes; sprinkle with almonds.

# Onion and Cheese Chicken Bake

TOTAL COOKING TIME: 13 minutes
Serves 6

- 2 tablespoons butter or margarine
- ½ teaspoon salt
- ½ teaspoon pepper
- 3 whole boneless chicken breasts, halved and skin removed
- 8 oz. fresh mushrooms, sliced
- 1 can (3 oz.) French fried onion rings
- ½ cup shredded Monterey Jack cheese

Melt butter in small bowl at HIGH for 1 to 1¼ minutes. Stir in salt and pepper. Arrange chicken in 12 × 8-in. baking dish with meatiest portions toward outside of dish. Pour seasoned butter over chicken. Cover with wax paper.

Microwave at HIGH for 5 minutes. Turn pieces over. Top with mushrooms. Cover with wax paper. Microwave at HIGH for 4 to 5 minutes, or until chicken is no longer pink. Top with French fried onion rings and cheese. Microwave at HIGH, uncovered, for 1 to 2 minutes, or until cheese melts.

## Chicken Divan ↑

Code: C-2 Medium
TOTAL COOKING TIME: 18 minutes
Serves 4

2 pkgs. (10 oz. each) frozen broccoli spears
1 can (10¾ oz.) condensed cream of
   chicken soup
¼ cup dairy sour cream
1 tablespoon lemon juice
1 teaspoon soy sauce
⅛ teaspoon garlic powder
2 cups cubed cooked chicken
1 tablespoon butter or margarine
⅓ cup grated Parmesan cheese
¼ cup dry unseasoned bread crumbs

Place broccoli packages in oven. Microwave at HIGH
for 3 minutes, or until package is flexible. Layer broccoli
in 12 × 8-in. baking dish. In medium bowl mix soup, sour
cream, lemon juice, soy sauce and garlic powder. Stir in
chicken; pour over broccoli. Set aside.

Melt butter in small bowl at HIGH for 45 to 60 seconds.
Stir in Parmesan cheese and bread crumbs. Sprinkle
over casserole. Cover with wax paper. Microwave at
HIGH for 12 to 14 minutes, or until hot.

## Turkey Tetrazzini

Code: C-1 Medium
TOTAL COOKING TIME: 23 minutes
Serves 4 to 6

1 pkg. (7 oz.) uncooked spaghetti
1 pkg. (10 oz.) frozen peas
2 cups chopped cooked turkey
1 can (10¾ oz.) condensed cream of
   mushroom soup
¼ cup half and half
⅛ teaspoon garlic powder
⅛ teaspoon pepper
¼ cup grated Parmesan cheese

Prepare spaghetti as directed, page 83. Place in 2-qt.
casserole. Place package of frozen peas in oven. Microwave at HIGH for 2 minutes. Drain. Add to spaghetti.
Mix in turkey, soup, half and half, garlic powder and
pepper. Microwave at HIGH for 5 minutes, stirring
once. Sprinkle with cheese. Microwave at HIGH for 5
to 6 minutes, or until heated through.

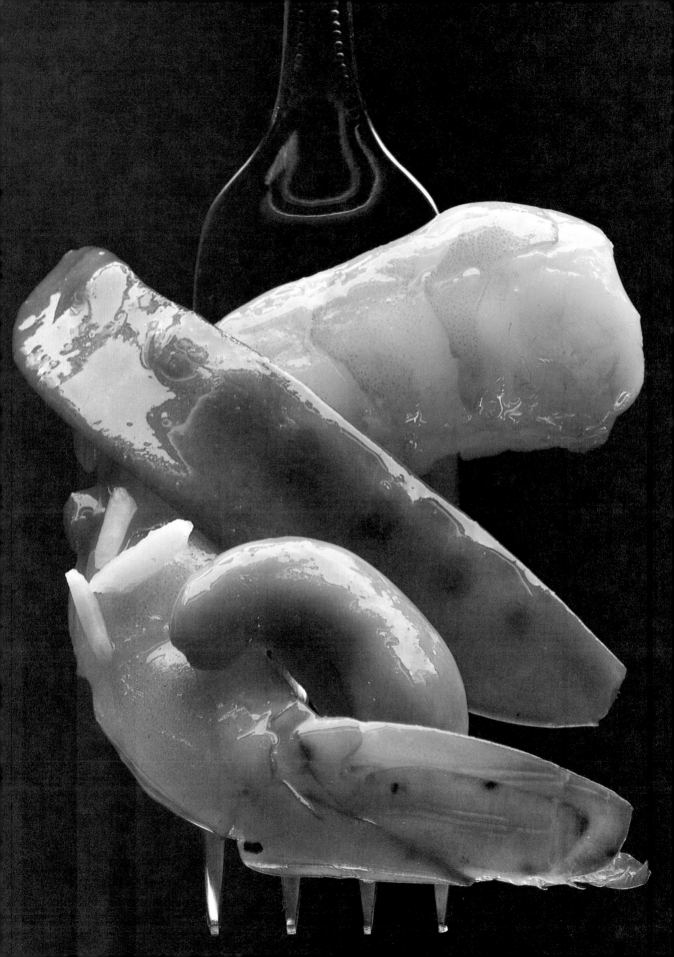

# Fish & Seafood

Fish and seafood are gaining in popularity all over the country. Many supermarkets are expanding their selection of fresh fish. High in protein and low in fat, fish and seafood are great favorites of nutrition-conscious consumers. The moist, quick cooking of microwave energy does wonders for the flavor and texture of these delicate foods. For best results, microwave just before serving time and watch carefully to avoid overcooking.

## How to Defrost Shrimp and Scallops

**Remove** packaging. Place seafood in baking dish or on roasting rack. Break apart if possible. Microwave as directed in chart, page 74, or until pliable, stirring 1 or 2 times. Rinse in cool water. Let stand for 2 to 3 minutes.

## How to Microwave Shrimp and Scallops

**Arrange** seafood in single layer in baking dish. Cover with plastic wrap. Microwave as directed in chart, page 74, or until opaque, stirring 1 or 2 times. Let stand, covered, for 1 to 2 minutes.

## How to Defrost Fish

**Remove** packaging. Place fish (fillets, steaks or small whole fish) on roasting rack. Shield thin parts with foil. Microwave for half the time as directed in chart, page 74. Turn fish over.

**Rearrange** so thickest parts are to outside and thinnest parts overlap. Remove shields. Microwave remaining time, or until pliable, but still cool. Let stand for 5 to 10 minutes.

## How to Microwave Fish

**Brush** fish (fillets, steaks or small whole fish) with melted butter or lemon juice or roll in crumbs, if desired. Place on roasting rack. Cover with wax paper (except crumb-coated fish).

**Microwave** for half the time as directed in chart, page 74. Rearrange fish, placing less cooked parts to the outside. Microwave remaining time, or until fish flakes. Let stand for 2 to 3 minutes.

Pictured: Chinese Shrimp, page 76

## DEFROSTING

NOTE: See page 4 for Auto Defrost instructions.

| ITEM | MICROWAVE TIME AT 4 | PROCEDURE |
|---|---|---|
| **Whole fish** | 4 to 7½ min./lb. | Follow photo directions, page 73. |
| **Steaks,** 1 inch thick | 3 to 5½ min./lb. | Follow photo directions, page 73. |
| **Fillets,** ¼ to 1 inch thick | 3 to 5 min./lb. | Follow photo directions, page 73. |
| **Shrimp** | 3 to 4 min./lb. | Follow photo directions, page 73. |
| **Scallops** | 3½ to 5½ min./lb. | Follow photo directions, page 73. |

## MICROWAVING

| ITEM | TOTAL TIME | POWER LEVEL | PROCEDURE |
|---|---|---|---|
| **Whole fish** | 8 to 12 min./lb. | 5 | Follow photo directions, page 73. |
| **Steaks** | 5 to 8 min./lb. | High | Follow photo directions, page 73. |
| **Fillets** | 2 to 5 min./lb. | High | Follow photo directions, page 73. |
| **Shrimp** | 3½ to 5 min./lb. | High | Follow photo directions, page 73. |
| **Scallops** | 3½ to 5 min./lb. | High | Follow photo directions, page 73. |

## Stuffed Trout

**Code: F-1 Medium**
TOTAL COOKING TIME: 18 minutes
Serves 4

- 4 slices bacon
- 1 cup cooked rice
- ¼ cup raisins
- 1 tablespoon snipped fresh parsley or 1½ teaspoons dried parsley flakes
- 1 teaspoon lemon juice
- ⅛ teaspoon dried tarragon leaves, optional
- 4 fresh drawn* stream trout

Place bacon in 12 × 8-in. baking dish. Microwave at HIGH for 4 to 5 minutes, or until crisp. Drain. Crumble. In medium bowl mix bacon, rice, raisins, parsley, lemon juice and tarragon.

Spoon one-fourth of stuffing into each fish. Place fish on baking sheet. Cover with wax paper. Microwave at 5 for 10 to 13 minutes, or until fish flakes easily near backbone, turning sheet once. Let stand for 2 minutes.

*Whole fish, gutted.

## Company Salmon

**Code: F-1 Rare**
TOTAL COOKING TIME: 24 minutes
Serves 4

- ½ cup finely chopped celery
- ¼ cup finely chopped onion
- ¼ cup butter or margarine
- ½ cup sliced fresh mushrooms
- ½ cup dry bread crumbs
- 2 tablespoons lemon juice
- 4 salmon steaks, 1-in. thick
  Paprika

In medium bowl combine celery, onion and butter. Cover. Microwave at HIGH for 2 minutes. Stir in mushrooms, bread crumbs and lemon juice. Set aside. Arrange steaks in 12 × 8-in. baking dish with narrow ends toward center. Cover with wax paper.

Microwave at 5 for 10 minutes. Turn steaks over. Spread one-fourth of crumb mixture over each steak. Microwave, uncovered, at 5 for 10 to 12 minutes, or until fish flakes easily with fork. Let stand for 3 minutes.

# Sole Almondine ↓

TOTAL COOKING TIME: 12 minutes
Serves 3 to 4

¼ cup butter or margarine
1 pkg. (2½ oz.) slivered almonds
1 tablespoon snipped fresh parsley or 1½
    teaspoons dried parsley flakes
⅛ teaspoon salt
⅛ teaspoon pepper
1 tablespoon lemon juice
1 lb. sole fillets, ¼-in. thick

Place butter in pie plate. Microwave at HIGH for 1¼ to 1½ minutes, or until butter melts. Stir in almonds. Microwave at HIGH for 5 to 6 minutes, or until almonds are golden brown, stirring 2 times during cooking. Stir in parsley, salt, pepper and lemon juice.

Arrange fillets in 12 × 8-in. baking dish with narrow ends toward center. Top with butter and almonds. Cover with plastic wrap. Microwave at HIGH for 3½ to 4½ minutes, or until fish flakes easily with fork, turning dish once. Let stand for 3 minutes.

# Halibut in Butter Sauce

Code: F-1 Medium
TOTAL COOKING TIME: 7½ minutes
Serves 4 to 6

3 tablespoons chopped onion
3 tablespoons butter or margarine
1 tablespoon snipped fresh parsley or 1½
    teaspoons dried parsley flakes
2 teaspoons lemon juice
½ teaspoon prepared mustard
⅛ teaspoon garlic powder
    Dash salt
1½ lbs. halibut fillets, ½-in. thick

In small bowl combine onion and butter. Microwave at HIGH for 1 to 1½ minutes, or until butter melts. Mix in parsley, lemon juice, mustard, garlic powder and salt.

Arrange fillets in 12 × 8-in. baking dish with narrow ends toward center. Spoon butter mixture over fillets. Cover with plastic wrap. Microwave at HIGH for 5 to 6 minutes, or until fish flakes easily with fork, turning dish once. Let stand for 3 minutes.

## Crêpes St. Jacques

TOTAL COOKING TIME: 14¾ minutes
Serves 4

1    cup sliced fresh mushrooms
2    cloves garlic, minced
5    tablespoons butter or margarine, divided
1    tablespoon lemon juice
1    lb. scallops, cut into bite-size pieces
3    tablespoons all-purpose flour
¼    teaspoon salt
⅛    teaspoon pepper
     Half and half
2    tablespoons white wine
8    large crêpes
     Dried parsley flakes

In large bowl combine mushrooms, garlic, 3 tablespoons butter and the lemon juice. Microwave at HIGH for 1½ to 2½ minutes, or until butter melts and mushrooms are tender, stirring after half the time. Stir in scallops. Reduce power to [7]. Microwave for 2½ to 3 minutes, or until opaque, stirring after each minute. Drain scallops and mushrooms, reserving liquid. Set aside.

Place remaining 2 tablespoons butter in 4-cup measure. Microwave at HIGH for 1 to 1¼ minutes, or until butter melts. Add flour, salt and pepper. Blend in reserved liquid. Add enough half and half to equal 1¾ cups. Reduce power to [7]. Microwave for 4 to 5½ minutes, or until thickened, stirring after the first 2 minutes and then after each minute. Stir wine into sauce.

Mix ¾ cup sauce into scallops and mushrooms. Spoon about ¼ cup scallop mixture down center of each crêpe. Fold in sides. Place in 12 × 8-in. baking dish. Pour remaining sauce over top. Sprinkle with parsley flakes. Cover with wax paper. Microwave at [8] for 1½ to 3 minutes, or until heated.

## Shrimp Scampi

Code: F-2 Medium
TOTAL COOKING TIME: 7 minutes
Serves 4

1    tablespoon snipped fresh parsley or 1½ teaspoons dried parsley flakes
1    large clove garlic, minced
¼    cup plus 2 tablespoons butter or margarine
1    tablespoon lemon juice
1    lb. raw medium shrimp, shelled and deveined
2    teaspoons grated Parmesan cheese

In 2-qt. casserole combine parsley, garlic, butter and lemon juice. Microwave at [7] for 2 minutes. Stir in shrimp and Parmesan cheese. Microwave at HIGH for 4 to 5 minutes, or until shrimp are opaque. Let stand for 2 to 3 minutes.

## Shrimp Creole

TOTAL COOKING TIME: 14 minutes
Serves 4 to 6

½    cup finely chopped onion
½    cup finely chopped green pepper
½    cup finely chopped celery
2    cloves garlic, minced
3    tablespoons butter or margarine
2    tablespoons cornstarch
1    can (16 oz.) stewed tomatoes
1    can (8 oz.) tomato sauce
1    tablespoon Worcestershire sauce
1    teaspoon chili powder
     Dash red pepper sauce
1    lb. raw medium shrimp, shelled and deveined
     Hot cooked rice

In 2-qt. casserole combine onion, green pepper, celery, garlic and butter. Microwave at HIGH for 5 minutes, or until tender-crisp, stirring once. Mix in cornstarch. Stir in stewed tomatoes, tomato sauce, Worcestershire sauce, chili powder and red pepper sauce. Cover.

Microwave at HIGH for 6 to 7 minutes, or until bubbly, stirring after half the time. Stir in shrimp. Cover. Microwave at HIGH for 2 minutes. Let stand for 5 minutes. Serve over rice.

## Chinese Shrimp

TOTAL COOKING TIME: 14½ minutes
Serves 4 to 6

1    pkg. (6 oz.) frozen pea pods
2    teaspoons cornstarch
½    cup water
1    teaspoon soy sauce
1    teaspoon instant chicken bouillon granules
½    teaspoon salt
1    cup sliced fresh mushrooms
1    cup thinly sliced celery
⅓    cup chopped green onion
1    lb. raw medium shrimp, shelled and deveined
½    cup roasted cashews
     Hot cooked rice

Place package of pea pods in oven. Microwave at HIGH for 1 minute. Set aside. In 2-qt. casserole blend cornstarch, water and soy sauce. Stir in bouillon granules and salt. Microwave at HIGH for 4 minutes to thicken, stirring 2 or 3 times. Add pea pods, mushrooms, celery and green onion. Microwave at HIGH for 5 minutes. Stir in shrimp and cashews. Microwave at HIGH for 3½ to 4½ minutes, or until shrimp are opaque, stirring 1 or 2 times. Serve over rice.

# Bouillabaisse ⌃

**Code: C-1 Medium**
TOTAL COOKING TIME: 30 minutes
Serves 6 to 8

- 12 clams in shell, scrubbed
- 1 lb. crab in shell, cut into 3-in. chunks
- 1 lb. fresh fish fillets, cut into 1½-in. chunks
- 1 lb. raw jumbo shrimp in shells
- 2 cans (16 oz. each) stewed tomatoes
- 2 bottles (8 oz. each) clam juice
- 2 cups hot water
- 1 green pepper, cut into 1-in. pieces
- 2 stalks celery, cut into ¼-in. slices

Soak clams in water for 2 hours; drain. Rinse all seafood except fillets well. Place in 5-qt. casserole. Add remaining ingredients; cover. Microwave at HIGH for 25 to 30 minutes, or until fish and seafood is opaque, stirring once. Let stand for 5 minutes.

# Eggs & Cheese

Easy to prepare and store, eggs and cheese are good, low cost
sources of protein for meatless meals. The microwave oven cooks these delicate
foods with impressive results. Scrambled eggs are fluffier and cheese creations are creamy
smooth. Be careful not to overcook eggs; they continue to cook during
standing time. Do not microwave eggs in the shell.

## How to Microwave Scrambled Eggs

**Place** butter in serving bowl or casserole as directed in chart, below. Microwave at HIGH for 45 seconds to 1¼ minutes, or until butter melts. Add eggs and milk, scrambling with fork.

**Microwave** at HIGH as directed in chart, below, breaking up and stirring eggs 2 times. (Eggs are done when they are still soft and moist.) Let stand for 1 to 4 minutes before serving.

**Scrambled Eggs With Green Pepper and Onion.** Follow photo directions above, adding 1 teaspoon finely chopped green pepper and 1 teaspoon finely chopped onion per egg. Combine butter, green pepper and onion in bowl. Microwave at HIGH for 45 seconds to 1½ minutes, or until tender-crisp. Continue as directed.

**Scrambled Eggs With Cheese and Ham.** Follow photo directions above, adding 1 tablespoon chopped fully cooked ham and 1 tablespoon shredded Cheddar cheese per egg. Melt butter as directed. Add ham with eggs and milk. Continue as directed. Quickly stir in cheese before standing time.

## Scrambled Egg Chart

| MICROWAVING | | | |
|---|---|---|---|
| EGGS | BUTTER | MILK | TIME |
| 2 | 1 tablespoon | 2 tablespoons | 1¼ to 1¾ minutes |
| 4 | 1 tablespoon | 2 tablespoons | 2 to 3 minutes |
| 6 | 2 tablespoons | ¼ cup | 3¼ to 4¼ minutes |

Pictured: Quiche Lorraine, page 80

# Quiche Lorraine (pictured on page 78)

**Manual: Hot**
TOTAL COOKING TIME: 29 minutes
Serves 6 to 8

- 1 **microwaved 9-in. Pastry Shell**
- 1 **cup shredded Swiss cheese**
- ¼ **cup chopped green onion**
- 3 **eggs**
- 1 **cup half and half**
- ¼ **teaspoon salt**
- ⅛ **teaspoon pepper**
- ⅛ **teaspoon garlic powder**
- 4 **slices bacon, cooked and crumbled, page 46**

Follow photo directions for microwaving quiche, below.

## Spinach Quiche

Follow the recipe above, substituting Monterey Jack cheese for Swiss cheese and 1 pkg. (10 oz.) frozen chopped spinach, defrosted and drained, for bacon. Top with 1 cup French fried onion rings, if desired. Microwave as directed.

NOTE: To defrost spinach, microwave at HIGH for 2 to 3 minutes, or until hot to the touch. Let stand to complete defrosting.

## Sausage and Mushroom Quiche

Follow the recipe at left, substituting mozzarella cheese for Swiss cheese and 1 cup cooked, crumbled pork sausage for bacon. Add 1 can (4 oz.) mushroom stems and pieces, drained, with cheese and green onion. Microwave as directed.

## Seafood Quiche

Follow the recipe at left, substituting 1 can (4¼ oz.) tiny shrimp, rinsed and drained, for bacon and ⅛ teaspoon red pepper for black pepper. Top with 1 cup French fried onion rings, if desired. Microwave as directed.

## *How to Microwave Quiche Lorraine*

**Prepare** pastry shell as directed, page 101. Sprinkle with cheese and onion. Set aside. In medium bowl beat eggs, half and half, salt, pepper and garlic powder.

**Microwave** at ⑤ for 5 to 6 minutes, or until mixture begins to thicken, stirring after the first 2 minutes and then after each minute.

**Pour** egg mixture into prepared crust. Sprinkle with crumbled bacon.

**Microwave** at ⑤ for 8 to 15 minutes, or until set (center will be slightly soft set), turning every 4 minutes. Let stand for 5 minutes.

# Cheese Omelet →

TOTAL COOKING TIME: 6¾ minutes
Serves 2

- 3 **eggs, separated**
- 3 **tablespoons half and half**
- ¼ **teaspoon baking powder**
- ¼ **teaspoon seasoned salt**
- ⅛ **teaspoon pepper**
- 1 **tablespoon butter or margarine**
- ½ **cup shredded Cheddar cheese**

In medium bowl beat egg whites until soft peaks form. Combine egg yolks, half and half, baking powder, salt and pepper; fold into beaten egg whites. Set aside.

Melt butter in 9-in. pie plate at HIGH for 45 to 60 seconds. Spread egg mixture in pie plate. Microwave at 5 for 4 to 6 minutes, or until center is set, running rubber spatula around edge of pie plate after half the time. Sprinkle with Cheddar cheese. Fold in half. Let stand for 1 minute.

# Swiss Fondue

Manual: Medium   Manual: Warm +
TOTAL COOKING TIME: 7 minutes
Serves 3 to 4

- 1 **clove garlic, cut in half**
- 1¼ **cups white wine**
- 3 **tablespoons all-purpose flour**
- ¼ **teaspoon salt**
  **Dash pepper**
  **Dash ground nutmeg**
- 3 **cups shredded Swiss cheese**
  **French bread cubes**

Rub inside of medium bowl with garlic; discard garlic. Add wine. Microwave at 8 for 2 to 3 minutes, or until very hot. In plastic bag combine flour, salt, pepper and nutmeg. Add cheese, tossing to coat. Stir into wine. Microwave at 8 for 3 to 4 minutes, or until smooth, stirring 2 or 3 times. Serve with bread cubes.

# Welsh Rarebit

Manual: Medium
TOTAL COOKING TIME: 8 minutes
Serves 4 to 6

- 1 **lb. pasteurized process cheese loaf,**
    **cut into cubes**
- ¾ **cup beer**
- 1 **teaspoon Worcestershire sauce**
- ½ **teaspoon dry mustard**
    **Bread cubes or slices**

Combine cheese, beer, Worcestershire sauce and dry mustard in medium bowl. Microwave at 5 for 7 to 8 minutes, or until smooth, stirring 2 or 3 times. Serve over bread.

# Baked Eggs in Hash

TOTAL COOKING TIME: 8½ minutes
Serves 2

- 1 **can (15 oz.) corned beef hash**
- 2 **eggs**
- ¼ **cup shredded Cheddar cheese, divided**
    **Salt**
    **Pepper**

Divide corned beef hash between two 10-oz. custard cups. With back of spoon make hollow in center of hash. Break egg into each hollow. Pierce yolks with wooden pick. Cover tightly with plastic wrap.

Microwave at 5 for 7½ to 8½ minutes, or until hash is hot and egg white is nearly opaque, turning cups once. Sprinkle 2 tablespoons cheese over each egg. Cover and let stand 1 minute. Salt and pepper each to taste.

# Pasta, Rice & Cereal

Pasta and rice microwave without worry of scorching or sticking, although they require about the same amount of cooking time as with conventional methods. The microwave is particularly adept at reheating pasta and rice with retention of moisture, texture and flavor. Hot cereal is so easy to microwave that a child can handle the preparation right in a serving bowl. It is simple to achieve a smooth texture with minimal clean-up.

## How to Microwave Pasta

**Combine** water, salt and oil in 12 × 8-in. baking dish for lasagna or 3-qt. casserole for macaroni, spaghetti or noodles. Cover and microwave at HIGH for 8 to 11 minutes, or until boiling.

**Add** pasta (macaroni, spaghetti, egg noodles or lasagna noodles). Microwave at HIGH as directed in chart, opposite, or until tender, stirring once. Drain.

## How to Microwave Long Grain or Short Grain Rice

**Combine** hot water, rice, salt and butter in 2-qt. casserole as directed in chart, opposite. Cover. Microwave at HIGH for 5 minutes. Stir. Cover.

**Microwave** at 7 as directed, or until rice is tender and liquid is absorbed, stirring once. Let stand, covered, for 5 minutes. Stir with fork.

## How to Microwave Cooked Cereal

**Combine** cereal, salt and hot water in bowl or casserole as directed in chart, opposite. Microwave at HIGH for half the time as directed.

**Stir.** Microwave remaining time, or until liquid is absorbed and cereal is desired consistency, stirring once. Let stand for 1 to 2 minutes. Stir before serving.

| | | | MICROWAVING | | |
|---|---|---|---|---|---|
| **PASTA** | **HOT WATER** | **SALT** | **OIL** | **MICROWAVE TIME** | **PROCEDURE** |
| **Lasagna noodles,** (8 oz. pkg.) | 6 cups | 1 tsp. | 1 tbsp. | 11 to 16 min. | Follow photo directions, opposite. Microwave, covered, until tender, stirring once. |
| **Elbow macaroni or spaghetti,** (7 oz. pkg.) | 6 cups | 1 tsp. | 1 tbsp. | 7 to 10 min. | Follow photo directions, opposite. Microwave, uncovered, until tender, stirring once. |
| **Egg noodles,** (3 cups) | 6 cups | 1 tsp. | 1 tbsp. | 8 to 10 min. | Follow photo directions, opposite. Microwave, uncovered, until tender, stirring once. |

| **RICE** | **HOT WATER** | **SALT** | **BUTTER** | **MICROWAVE TIME** | **PROCEDURE** |
|---|---|---|---|---|---|
| **1 cup long or short grain rice** | 2 cups | 1 tsp. | 1 tsp. | High 5 min., then 7, 9 to 11 min. | Follow photo directions, opposite. |
| **1½ cups instant rice** | 1½ cups | ½ tsp. | 1 tsp. | High 3 to 4 min. | In 1-qt. casserole combine water, salt and butter. Microwave until boiling. Stir in rice; cover. Let stand for 5 minutes, or until rice is tender and liquid is absorbed. Stir with fork. |

| **CEREAL** | **BOWL SIZE** | **CEREAL** | **SALT** | **HOT WATER** | **MICROWAVE TIME** | **PROCEDURE** |
|---|---|---|---|---|---|---|
| **Quick oatmeal,** | | | | | | Follow photo directions, opposite. |
| 1 serving | 1-qt. | ⅓ cup | ⅛ tsp. | ¾ cup | 2 to 3 min. | |
| 2 servings | 1- to 1½-qt. | ⅔ cup | ¼ tsp. | 1½ cups | 4 to 5 min. | |
| 4 servings | 2-qt. | 1⅓ cups | ½ tsp. | 3 cups | 6 to 7 min. | |
| **Old-fashioned oatmeal,** | | | | | | Follow photo directions, opposite. |
| 1 serving | 1-qt. | ⅓ cup | ⅛ tsp. | ¾ cup | 4 to 6 min. | |
| 2 servings | 1- to 1½-qt. | ⅔ cup | ¼ tsp. | 1⅓ cups | 5 to 7 min. | |
| 4 servings | 2-qt. | 1⅓ cups | ½ tsp. | 2½ cups | 8 to 9 min. | |
| **Regular cream of wheat,** | | | | | | Follow photo directions, opposite. |
| 1 serving | 1-qt. | 2½ tbsp. | ⅛ tsp. | 1 cup | 4 to 6 min. | |
| 2 servings | 2-qt. | ⅓ cup | ¼ tsp. | 1¾ cups | 5½ to 7½ min. | |
| 4 servings | 3-qt. | ⅔ cup | ½ tsp. | 3½ cups | 9 to 12 min. | |
| **Quick cream of wheat,** | | | | | | Follow photo directions, opposite. |
| 1 serving | 1-qt. | 2½ tbsp. | ⅛ tsp. | 1 cup | 2 to 3 min. | |
| 2 servings | 2-qt. | ⅓ cup | ¼ tsp. | 1¾ cups | 3 to 4 min. | |
| 4 servings | 3-qt. | ⅔ cup | ½ tsp. | 3½ cups | 6 to 7 min. | |
| **Instant cream of wheat,** | | | | | | Follow photo directions, opposite. |
| 1 serving | 1-qt. | 2½ tbsp. | ⅛ tsp. | ¾ cup | 1½ to 2½ min. | |
| 2 servings | 2-qt. | ⅓ cup | ¼ tsp. | 1⅓ cups | 2½ to 3½ min. | |
| 4 servings | 3-qt. | ⅔ cup | ½ tsp. | 2¾ cups | 4½ to 6 min. | |

## Noodles Almondine

TOTAL COOKING TIME: 24 minutes
Serves 4 to 6

- ¼ cup plus 1 tablespoon butter or margarine, divided
- ¼ cup slivered almonds
- 3 cups uncooked medium egg noodles
- ¼ cup grated Parmesan cheese
- 2 tablespoons snipped fresh parsley or
  1 tablespoon dried parsley flakes

Place 1 tablespoon butter in pie plate. Microwave at HIGH for 45 to 60 seconds, or until butter melts. Stir in almonds. Microwave at HIGH for 7 to 8 minutes, or until light golden brown, stirring 2 times. Set aside.

Prepare noodles as directed, page 83. Drain. Place in 2-qt. casserole. Add almonds, Parmesan cheese, remaining ¼ cup butter and the parsley, stirring to coat. Microwave at 5 for 2 to 4 minutes, or until heated and butter melts, stirring once.

### Poppy Seed Noodles
Follow the recipe above, substituting 1 tablespoon poppy seed for almonds and 1 tablespoon butter.

## Macaroni and Cheese

TOTAL COOKING TIME: 18 minutes
Serves 4

- 1 pkg. (7 oz.) uncooked macaroni
- 2 tablespoons butter or margarine
- 2 tablespoons all-purpose flour
- ½ teaspoon salt
- ⅛ teaspoon pepper
- ½ teaspoon Worcestershire sauce
- ½ teaspoon prepared mustard
- 1 cup milk
- 2 cups shredded Cheddar cheese

Prepare macaroni as directed, page 83. Drain. Place in 2-qt. casserole. Set aside. Place butter in 1-qt. casserole. Microwave at HIGH for 1 to 1¼ minutes, or until butter melts. Stir in flour, salt, pepper, Worcestershire sauce and mustard. Blend in milk. Microwave at 7 for 4 to 6 minutes, or until thickened, stirring 2 times. Add cheese, stirring until cheese melts. Mix into cooked macaroni. Cover. Microwave at HIGH for 5 minutes.

## Cheesy Rice

Code: V-8 Medium
TOTAL COOKING TIME: 16 minutes
Serves 4 to 6

- 2 cups hot water
- 1 cup long grain rice
- ½ teaspoon salt
- ⅛ teaspoon garlic powder
- 2 cups shredded Cheddar cheese
- ¼ cup grated Parmesan cheese
- ¼ cup slivered almonds
- 1 tablespoon snipped fresh parsley or
  1½ teaspoons dried parsley flakes

In 2-qt. casserole combine hot water, rice, salt and garlic powder. Cover. Microwave at HIGH for 5 minutes. Reduce power to 7. Microwave for 9 to 11 minutes, or until liquid is absorbed and rice is tender, stirring once. Stir in Cheddar and Parmesan cheese, almonds and parsley. Let stand, covered, for 5 minutes. Stir before serving.

## Confetti Rice ↑

Code: V-9 Medium
TOTAL COOKING TIME: 28 minutes
Serves 6

½ cup chopped onion
3 tablespoons butter or margarine
2 cups hot water
1 cup long grain rice
1 pkg. (10 oz.) frozen peas and carrots
½ cup sliced fresh mushrooms
2 teaspoons instant chicken bouillon granules
¼ teaspoon salt
⅛ teaspoon pepper

In 2-qt. casserole combine onion and butter. Microwave at HIGH for 4 minutes. Stir in remaining ingredients. Cover. Microwave at HIGH for 5 minutes. Stir; re-cover. Reduce power to ⑦. Microwave for 17 to 19 minutes, or until liquid is absorbed and rice is tender, stirring once. Let stand for 5 minutes. Stir before serving.

## Curried Rice

Code: V-8 Medium
TOTAL COOKING TIME: 18 minutes
Serves 4 to 6

¼ cup chopped onion
¼ cup chopped green pepper
2 tablespoons butter or margarine
2 cups hot water
1 cup long grain rice
1 teaspoon curry powder
¾ teaspoon salt

In 2-qt. casserole combine onion, green pepper and butter. Cover. Microwave at HIGH for 2 minutes. Add remaining ingredients. Cover. Microwave at HIGH for 5 minutes. Reduce power to ⑦. Microwave for 9 to 11 minutes, or until liquid is absorbed and rice is tender, stirring once. Let stand, covered, for 5 minutes. Stir before serving.

### Yellow Rice
Follow the recipe above, substituting ½ teaspoon ground turmeric for curry powder.

# Vegetables & Fruit

Vegetables and fruit are excellent sources of important nutrients and fiber, and add color and texture to your meal. Microwaving helps preserve water-soluble vitamins and minerals; they don't cook away in added liquid as in conventional cooking. Flavor, texture and color of vegetables and fruit are also retained during microwaving. Jams and jellies are simple to make in the microwave, too.

## How to Microwave Vegetables and Fruit

**Cut** fruits and vegetables into uniform pieces for even cooking. Large pieces take longer to cook than small ones. Rearrange large items during cooking and allow ample standing time.

**Quantity** affects cooking time. Be sure to increase the cooking time when increasing the quantity of food. When doubling the amount, increase cooking time by half. Rearrange or stir larger quantities more often.

**Rearrange or stir** vegetables and fruit for more even cooking. Small, cut-up pieces should be stirred from outside to center midway during cooking. Large, whole fruits or vegetables should be turned over or rearranged after half the cooking time.

**Standing time** allows the center portion of larger vegetables and fruits to tenderize. Microwaving until the center is tender results in an overcooked exterior.

## How to Microwave Broccoli or Asparagus Spears

**Arrange** broccoli or asparagus spears in single layer in 12 × 8-in. baking dish with stem ends towards outside of dish. Add ¼ cup water. Cover with plastic wrap.

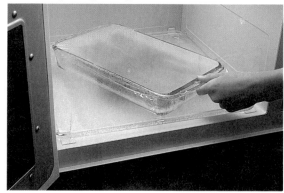

**Microwave** as directed in chart, page 92, or until tender-crisp, turning dish once. Let stand, covered, for 2 to 3 minutes.

## How to Microwave Cut Green Beans

**Place** cut green beans and ¼ cup water in casserole. Cover. Microwave as directed in chart, page 92, or until tender, stirring 1 or 2 times. Let stand, covered, for 2 to 3 minutes.

## How to Microwave Sliced Carrots

**Place** sliced carrots and 3 tablespoons water in 1-qt. casserole; cover. Microwave as directed in chart, page 92, or until hot or tender-crisp, stirring 1 or 2 times. Let stand, covered, for 3 minutes.

## How to Microwave Cauliflowerets

**Place** cauliflowerets and 2 tablespoons water in 1-qt. casserole; cover.

**Microwave** as directed in chart, page 92, or until tender-crisp, stirring 1 or 2 times. Let stand, covered, for 3 minutes.

## How to Microwave Corn on the Cob

**Remove** husk and corn silk from fresh corn, if desired. Wrap each ear of husked corn in plastic wrap or place in baking dish covered with plastic wrap. Ears in the husk can be placed directly on the oven floor.

**Microwave** as directed in chart, page 92, or until tender, rearranging 1 or 2 times. Let stand, covered, for 5 minutes. Carefully remove plastic wrap or husk and silk to avoid steam.

## How to Microwave Winter Squash

**Pierce** squash 2 times. Microwave as directed in chart, page 92, or until tender, rearranging once.

**Let stand** for 5 to 10 minutes. Cut in half; scoop out seeds and discard. Spoon out squash. Mash, if desired.

## How to Microwave Baked Potatoes

**Pierce** each potato twice with fork. Place in oven on paper towel. Microwave as directed in chart, page 92, or until soft to the touch, rearranging once.

**Wrap** in foil or place in covered casserole. Let stand for 5 minutes. (Potatoes will retain heat for 20 minutes.)

## How to Microwave Frozen Boxed Vegetables

**Remove** vegetable from package. Place in 1-qt. casserole with 2 tablespoons water.

**Microwave**, covered, as directed in chart, page 92, stirring once. Let stand, covered, for 2 minutes.

## How to Microwave Frozen Vegetable Pouches

**Remove** pouch from box. Cut a slit in one side of pouch. Place in 1-qt. casserole or serving bowl.

**Microwave** as directed in chart, page 92, flexing pouch once. Let stand for 2 minutes. Empty vegetables into casserole or serving bowl.

## How to Microwave Canned Vegetables

**Drain** all but 1 tablespoon liquid from vegetables. Place liquid and vegetables in 1-qt. casserole.

**Microwave**, covered, as directed in chart, page 92, or until hot, stirring once.

## How to Microwave Baked Apples

**Core** four medium apples and peel skin from top halves. Arrange in 8 × 8-in. baking dish or individual dishes.

**Fill** centers with brown sugar and cinnamon, if desired. Microwave as directed in chart, page 92, or until tender, turning 2 times. Let stand for 3 to 5 minutes.

## How to Microwave Baked Pears

**Halve** and core two medium pears. Place in 8 × 8-in. baking dish with narrow ends toward center. Fill centers with brown sugar and butter, if desired.

**Cover** dish with plastic wrap. Microwave as directed in chart, page 92, or until tender, turning dish once. Let stand, covered, for 2 to 3 minutes.

## How to Peel Peaches, Apricots, Nectarines and Tomatoes

**Measure** 4 cups water into bowl or 3-qt. casserole. Microwave at HIGH for 8 to 11 minutes, or until water boils. Add several pieces of fruit.

**Let stand**, covered with water, for 1 to 1½ minutes to loosen skin. Immerse fruit in cold water; peel. Repeat with any remaining fruit.

| | MICROWAVING | |
|---|---|---|
| | Weights given are purchase weights. | |

| ITEM | MICROWAVE TIME AT HIGH | PROCEDURE |
|---|---|---|
| **Apples,** | | |
| Baked (4) | 8 to 13 min. at 8 | Follow photo directions, page 91. |
| **Artichokes,** | | |
| Fresh | | |
| 2 | 5½ to 8½ min. | Place trimmed artichokes in 8 × 8-in. baking dish with ¼ cup water; cover with plastic wrap. Microwave until lower leaves can be pulled off and base pierces easily, rearranging once. Let stand for 3 minutes. |
| 4 | 9½ to 14½ min. | |
| **Asparagus spears,** | | |
| Fresh (1 lb.) | 6½ to 9½ min. | Follow photo directions, page 88. |
| Frozen (10 oz.) | 5 to 7 min. | Follow photo directions, page 90. |
| **Beans,** cut, | | |
| Fresh, green and wax | | |
| (1 lb.) | 8 to 13 min. | Follow photo directions, page 88. |
| (½ lb.) | 5 to 9 min. | Follow photo directions, page 88. |
| Frozen, green | | |
| (9 oz.) | 5 to 8 min. | Follow photo directions, page 90. |
| Frozen, lima | | |
| (10 oz.) | 5 to 7 min. | Follow photo directions, page 90. |
| **Broccoli,** | | |
| Fresh (1½ lbs.) | 8 to 12 min. | Follow photo directions, page 88. |
| frozen, spears or chopped | | |
| (10 oz.) | 5 to 7 min. | Follow photo directions, page 90. |
| Frozen pouch | 5 to 7½ min. | Follow photo directions, page 90. |
| (10 oz.) | | |
| **Brussels sprouts,** | | |
| Fresh (4 cups) | 5 to 9 min. | Place Brussels sprouts in 1½-qt. casserole with ¼ cup water. Microwave, covered, until tender-crisp. Let stand, covered, for 2 to 3 minutes. |
| Frozen (10 oz.) | 5 to 8 min. | Follow photo directions, page 90. |
| **Cabbage,** | | |
| Shredded (1 lb.) | 9 to 13½ min. | Place cabbage in 1½-qt. casserole with 2 tablespoons water. Microwave, covered, until tender-crisp. Let stand, covered, for 2 to 3 minutes. |
| Wedges (1 lb.) | 12½ to 15½ min. | Place cabbage in 12 × 8-in. baking dish with ¼ cup water. Microwave, covered, ·until tender-crisp. Let stand, covered, for 2 to 3 minutes. |
| **Canned (any vegetable),** | | |
| (15- to 16-oz. can) | 2 to 4 min. | Follow photo directions, page 90. |
| **Carrots,** slices or 1-in. pieces | | |
| Fresh (2 cups) | 4 to 8 min. | Follow photo directions, page 88. |
| Frozen (2 cups) | 5 to 7 min. | Follow photo directions, page 90. |

| ITEM | MICROWAVE TIME AT HIGH | PROCEDURE |
|---|---|---|
| **Cauliflower,** | | |
| Fresh, whole | | |
| (1 lb.) | 5½ to 7½ min. | Rinse. Wrap in plastic wrap. Microwave until tender-crisp, turning over after 3 minutes. Let stand, wrapped, for 2 to 3 minutes. |
| Fresh, flowerets | | |
| (2 cups) | 5 to 7 min. | Follow photo directions, page 88. |
| Frozen, flowerets | | |
| (10 oz.) | 5 to 7 min. | Follow photo directions, page 90. |
| **Corn,** | | |
| Fresh, on the cob | | |
| 2 | 7 to 10 min. | Follow photo directions, page 89. |
| 4 | 12 to 16 min. | Follow photo directions, page 89. |
| Frozen, on the cob | | |
| 2 | 5½ to 7½ min. | Follow photo directions, page 89. |
| 4 | 8 to 12½ min. | Follow photo directions, page 89. |
| Frozen, kernels | | |
| (10 oz.) | 4 to 6 min. | Follow photo directions, page 90. |
| **Pears,** | | |
| Baked (2) | 8 to 13 min. at [8] | Follow photo directions, page 91. |
| **Peas, green** | | |
| Frozen (10 oz.) | 5 to 7 min. | Follow photo directions, page 90. |
| Pouch (10 oz.) | 5 to 6 min. | Follow photo directions, page 90. |
| **Potatoes,** | | |
| Whole, new (8) | 5 to 9 min. | Scrub potatoes; do not peel. Pierce 2 times with fork. Place in 1½-qt. casserole with 2 tablespoons water. Microwave, covered, until tender. Let stand, covered, for 2 to 3 minutes. |
| White, med. (2 to 3, cut up) | | |
| Sweet | | |
| 2 (med.) | 6 to 10 min. | Follow photo directions, page 89. |
| 4 (med.) | 8½ to 13 min. | Follow photo directions, page 89. |
| Baking | | |
| 2 (med.) | 6 to 10 min. | Follow photo directions, page 89. |
| 4 (med.) | 10½ to 13 min. | Follow photo directions, page 89. |
| **Spinach,** | | |
| Fresh (1 lb.) | 5 to 8 min. | Place in 3-qt. casserole with 2 tablespoons water. Microwave, covered, until tender. Let stand, covered, for 2 to 3 minutes. |
| Frozen, leaf or chopped | | |
| (10 oz.) | 7 to 9 min. | Follow photo directions, page 90. |
| **Squash,** | | |
| Fresh, acorn | | |
| 1 whole | 8½ to 11 min. | Follow photo directions, page 89. |
| 2 whole | 13 to 16 min. | Follow photo directions, page 89. |
| Fresh, zucchini slices | | |
| (2 cups) (about 1 lb.) | 3 to 5 min. | Place zucchini slices and 2 tablespoons butter in 2-qt. casserole. Microwave, covered, until tender. Let stand, covered, for 2 to 3 minutes. |

## Cheesy Cauliflower

Code: V-2 Medium, S-5 Medium
TOTAL COOKING TIME: 16 minutes
Serves 4

- 1 small head cauliflower (about 1 lb.), separated into flowerets
- 1 tablespoon water
- 2 tablespoons butter or margarine
- 2 tablespoons all-purpose flour
- ¼ teaspoon salt
- ⅛ teaspoon pepper
- 1 cup milk
- 1 teaspoon Worcestershire sauce
- ½ cup shredded Swiss cheese
- 1 tablespoon snipped fresh parsley or 1½ teaspoons dried parsley flakes

In 2-qt. casserole place cauliflowerets and water. Cover. Microwave at HIGH for 7 to 8 minutes, or until fork tender, stirring once. Drain. Cover; set aside.

Place butter in 4-cup measure. Microwave at HIGH for 1 to 1¼ minutes, or until butter melts. Stir in flour, salt and pepper. Add milk and Worcestershire sauce. Microwave at HIGH for 3 to 4 minutes, or until thickened, stirring after first 2 minutes, and then after each minute. Stir in cheese and parsley. Pour over cauliflowerets.

## Broccoli Au Gratin

TOTAL COOKING TIME: 17 minutes
Serves 4

- 1 pkg. (10 oz.) frozen broccoli spears
- ¼ cup butter or margarine, divided
- 2 tablespoons all-purpose flour
- ¼ teaspoon salt
- ⅛ teaspoon pepper
- 1 cup milk
- ½ cup shredded Swiss or Cheddar cheese
- ⅓ cup seasoned bread crumbs

Remove outer wrapper from broccoli package. Place package on plate. Microwave at HIGH for 6 minutes, turning over after half the time and flexing package to break spears apart. Set aside.

Place 2 tablespoons butter in 1-qt. casserole. Microwave at HIGH for 1 to 1¼ minutes, or until butter melts. Stir in flour, salt and pepper. Blend in milk. Microwave at 7 for 4 to 6 minutes, or until thickened, stirring after first 2 minutes, and then after every minute. Stir in cheese. Add broccoli, stirring to coat.

Place remaining 2 tablespoons butter in custard cup or small bowl. Microwave at HIGH for 1 to 1¼ minutes, or until butter melts. Stir in bread crumbs. Sprinkle butter and crumb mixture over broccoli. Microwave at HIGH for 2 minutes.

## Glazed Carrots ↑

Code: V-3 Medium
TOTAL COOKING TIME: 9½ minutes
Serves 4

- 2 tablespoons butter or margarine
- 2 tablespoons packed brown sugar
- 1 lb. carrots, peeled and cut into 1-in. pieces

Place butter in small bowl or 1-cup measure. Microwave at HIGH for 1 to 1¼ minutes, or until butter melts. Mix in brown sugar. Place carrots in 1-qt. casserole. Pour butter and brown sugar mixture over carrots, tossing to coat. Cover. Microwave at HIGH for 6 to 8 minutes, or until carrots are fork tender, stirring after half the time.

## Scalloped Potatoes ↑

TOTAL COOKING TIME: 24 minutes
Serves 4

  3  **tablespoons butter or margarine**
 ½  **cup chopped onion**
  3  **tablespoons all-purpose flour**
 ½  **teaspoon salt**
 ⅛  **teaspoon pepper**
1½  **cups milk**
  4  **medium potatoes, peeled**

In 2-qt. casserole combine butter and onion. Microwave at HIGH for 1 to 2 minutes, or until butter melts. Stir in flour, salt and pepper. Blend in milk. Microwave at HIGH for 5 to 7 minutes, or until thickened, stirring after first 2 minutes, and then after every minute.

Cut potatoes in half lengthwise, then crosswise into ¼-in. slices. Add to thickened sauce. Cover. Microwave at HIGH for 10 to 15 minutes, or until potatoes are fork tender, stirring every 5 minutes. Let stand, covered, for 5 minutes.

### Au Gratin Potatoes
Follow the recipe above, adding 1 cup shredded Cheddar cheese to thickened white sauce.

## German Potato Salad

TOTAL COOKING TIME: 15½ minutes
Serves 4

  4  **medium red potatoes, peeled**
 ¼  **cup water**
  3  **slices bacon, cut up**
 ½  **cup chopped onion**
 ⅓  **cup chopped celery**
  1  **tablespoon all-purpose flour**
  1  **tablespoon sugar**
 ¼  **teaspoon salt**
 ⅛  **teaspoon pepper**
 ¼  **cup vinegar**
 ¼  **cup water**

Cut potatoes in half lengthwise, then crosswise into ¼-in. slices. In 2-qt. casserole combine potatoes and ¼ cup water. Cover. Microwave at HIGH for 7 to 9 minutes, or until potatoes are fork tender, stirring after half the time. Drain. Cover and set aside.

In small bowl or 1-qt. casserole combine bacon, onion and celery. Microwave at HIGH for 1½ to 2½ minutes, or until onion is tender, stirring after half the time. Mix in remaining ingredients. Microwave at HIGH for 1½ to 2 minutes, or until thickened, stirring after half the time. Add to potatoes, tossing to coat. Cover. Microwave at HIGH for 2 minutes.

### ← Apple Betty

TOTAL COOKING TIME: 15½ minutes
Serves 4 to 6

- ⅓ cup packed brown sugar
- ⅓ cup granulated sugar
- ¼ cup all-purpose flour
- 1 teaspoon ground cinnamon
- ½ teaspoon ground cardamom
- 6 cups sliced apples
- 2 tablespoons lemon juice

TOPPING:
- 3 tablespoons butter or margarine
- ½ cup dry unseasoned bread crumbs
- ⅛ teaspoon ground cinnamon

In large bowl combine brown sugar, granulated sugar, flour, 1 teaspoon cinnamon and the cardamom. Add apple slices and lemon juice, stirring to coat. Spoon into 2-qt. casserole.

In small bowl microwave butter at HIGH for 1 to 1¼ minutes, or until butter melts. Stir in bread crumbs and ⅛ teaspoon cinnamon. Sprinkle over apples.

Microwave at HIGH for 10 to 14 minutes, or until apples in center are tender, turning casserole once. Let stand for 2 minutes. Serve with cream, if desired.

### Baked Apples

Code: V-1 Hot
TOTAL COOKING TIME: 13 minutes
Serves 4

- 4 baking apples
- ¼ cup packed brown sugar
- ¼ cup raisins
- 3 tablespoons slivered almonds
- ¾ teaspoon ground cinnamon
- 4 teaspoons butter or margarine, divided

Core apples and peel skin from top half of each. Arrange in 8 × 8-in. baking dish. Combine brown sugar, raisins, almonds and cinnamon. Fill center of each apple with about one-fourth of sugar mixture. Dot each apple with 1 teaspoon butter. Microwave at **8** for 8 to 13 minutes, or until apples are tender, turning dish 2 times. Let stand for 5 minutes.

## Peach Melba

Manual: Hot
TOTAL COOKING TIME: 5½ minutes
Serves 4

  1  can (16 oz.) peach slices
  1  pkg. (10 oz.) frozen strawberries, defrosted
  ½  cup currant jelly
  1  tablespoon cornstarch

Drain syrup from fruit into 1-qt. casserole. Stir in jelly and cornstarch. Microwave at HIGH for 5 to 5½ minutes, or until thickened, stirring 2 times. Stir fruit into hot sauce. Serve over pound cake, if desired.

## Bananas Royale

TOTAL COOKING TIME: 6 minutes
Serves 4

  ¼  cup butter or margarine
  ¼  cup packed brown sugar
  ¼  cup whipping cream
  ¼  teaspoon ground cinnamon
  ¼  teaspoon ground nutmeg
  4  bananas, peeled and sliced
  ¼  cup brandy
     Vanilla ice cream

Place butter in casserole. Microwave at HIGH for 1¼ to 1½ minutes, or until butter melts. Stir in sugar, cream, cinnamon and nutmeg. Microwave at HIGH for 2 minutes. Add sliced bananas, stirring to coat. Microwave at HIGH for 2 minutes, stirring once. Warm brandy in 1-cup measure at HIGH for 30 seconds. Pour brandy over bananas; flame. Serve over vanilla ice cream.

## Cherries Jubilee

Manual: Hot
TOTAL COOKING TIME: 6½ minutes
Serves 4

  1  can (16 oz.) dark pitted cherries, drained, syrup reserved
  ¼  cup currant jelly
  1  tablespoon cornstarch
  ¼  cup cherry brandy
     Vanilla ice cream

In 1½-qt. casserole blend cherry syrup, jelly and cornstarch. Microwave at HIGH for 3 to 4 minutes, or until slightly thickened, stirring 2 times. Add cherries. Microwave at HIGH for 2 minutes. Place brandy in 1-cup measure. Microwave at HIGH for 30 seconds. Pour over hot cherry sauce; flame. Serve over vanilla ice cream.

## Applesauce

Code: V-1 Hot
TOTAL COOKING TIME: 14 minutes
Serves 3

  7  cups chopped peeled apples
  2  tablespoons water
  ½  teaspoon ground cinnamon
  ¼  teaspoon ground nutmeg
  2  to 3 tablespoons sugar

Combine all ingredients in 2-qt. casserole. Cover. Microwave at HIGH for 13 to 14 minutes, or until tender, stirring 2 times. Purée, if desired. Serve warm or cold.

## Strawberry Jam →

TOTAL COOKING TIME: 22 minutes
Makes 4 pints

- 2 pints sliced fresh strawberries (about 6 cups)
- 3 cups sugar
- 2 teaspoons grated lemon peel
- ¼ cup lemon juice
- 1 pkg. (6 oz.) strawberry-flavored gelatin

In 2-qt. bowl lightly crush berries. Add sugar, lemon peel and juice. Stir. Microwave at HIGH for 10 to 12 minutes, or until mixture reaches full boil, stirring occasionally. Reduce power to ⑤. Microwave for 10 minutes to simmer, stirring occasionally.

Stir in gelatin. Let stand for 30 minutes. Spoon into plastic freezer containers, leaving ½ inch at the top. Let stand until room temperature. Cover with lids. (Jam will thicken when cool.) Store in refrigerator or freezer.

## Fruit Compote

Manual: Warm +
TOTAL COOKING TIME: 7 minutes
Serves 4 to 6

- 1 can (8 oz.) sliced peaches, drained, 2 tablespoons syrup reserved
- 1 can (8 oz.) apricot halves, drained, 2 tablespoons syrup reserved
- ⅛ teaspoon ground cloves
- ⅛ teaspoon ground cinnamon
  Dash ground allspice
- 1 can (8 oz.) whole cranberry sauce
- 2 medium apples, peeled, cored and cut into 1½-in. pieces

In 1½-qt. casserole stir reserved syrups, cloves, cinnamon and allspice. Stir in cranberry sauce, peaches, apricots and apples. Cover. Microwave at HIGH for 6 to 7 minutes, or until hot, stirring after half the time. Serve warm or chilled.

## Stewed Fruit

Code: C-1 Medium
TOTAL COOKING TIME: 18 minutes
Serves 4 to 6

- 1 lb. mixed dried fruit
- 2 cups water
- ½ cup white wine

In 3-qt. casserole combine fruit, water and wine; soak for 30 minutes. Cover. Microwave at ⑦ for 15 to 18 minutes, or until fruit is plump and tender, stirring once. Let stand for 5 minutes.

# Desserts

Desserts add that special final touch to your meal. Microwaving makes almost any dessert easier to prepare, and the results are rich, moist and tender. Use the following recipes as a guide for adapting other favorites. And don't forget to use the microwave to reheat desserts that are best served warm.

## Dessert Chart

| ITEM | MICROWAVE TIME | POWER LEVEL | PROCEDURE |
|---|---|---|---|
| | **MICROWAVING** | | |
| **Cake layer** | 5 min.<br>2 to 5 min. | 7<br>High | Follow photo directions, page 104. |
| **Ring cake** | 10 min.<br>1½ to 3 min. | 7<br>High | Grease ring cake dish. Sprinkle with graham cracker crumbs or sugar, if desired. Add batter. Microwave at 7 for 10 minutes. Increase power to HIGH. Microwave until top springs back when touched lightly, turning dish 2 or 3 times. Let stand on counter for 10 minutes. |
| **One-crust pastry shell** | 6 to 8 min. | 7 | Follow photo directions, below. |
| **Pudding mix,**<br>1½ to 4⅛ oz. pkg.<br>4½ to 6⅛ oz. pkg. | 9½ to 12 min.<br>11 to 14 min. | 8<br>8 | Blend milk and pudding mix in 2-qt. casserole. Microwave until thick, stirring 2 or 3 times. |

## Pastry Shell

TOTAL COOKING TIME: 8 minutes
Makes 9-in. pastry shell

    1  cup all-purpose flour
1½  teaspoons sugar, optional
¼   teaspoon salt
⅓   cup shortening
3   tablespoons cold water
3   drops yellow food coloring

### How to Microwave Pastry Shell

**Combine** flour, sugar and salt. Cut in shortening until particles resemble coarse crumbs. Combine water and food coloring. Sprinkle over flour mixture, stirring with fork until particles are just moist enough to cling together and form a ball.

**Flatten** pastry into 6-in. circle. Wrap in plastic wrap and refrigerate for 30 minutes. Roll out on lightly floured board to fit 9-in. pie plate. Carefully fit into plate.

**Fold** edge to form high-standing rim; flute. Prick bottom and sides generously with fork. Microwave at 7 for 6 to 8 minutes, or until pastry appears dry and opaque, turning every 2 minutes.

Pictured: Pecan Pie, page 102

# Pecan Pie (pictured on page 100)

Manual: Hot
TOTAL COOKING TIME: 24 minutes
Makes 9-in. pie

- 1 microwaved 9-in. Pastry Shell
- ¼ cup butter or margarine
- 1 cup light corn syrup
- 3 eggs
- ½ cup packed dark brown sugar
- 1 teaspoon vanilla
- ¼ teaspoon salt
- 1⅓ cups chopped pecans

Prepare pastry shell as directed, page 101. Set aside. Place butter in 4-cup measure. Microwave at HIGH for 1¼ to 1½ minutes, or until butter melts. Blend in remaining ingredients one at a time. Pour into prepared pastry shell. Microwave at 5 for 14 to 15 minutes, or until set, turning after half the time. Cool.

# Pumpkin Pie

Manual: Hot
TOTAL COOKING TIME: 31 minutes
Makes 9-in. pie

- 1 microwaved 9-in. Pastry Shell
- 1 can (16 oz.) pumpkin
- 1 can (14 oz.) sweetened condensed milk
- 2 eggs
- 2 teaspoons pumpkin pie spice

Prepare pastry shell as directed, page 101. Set aside. In medium bowl blend pumpkin, condensed milk, eggs and spice. Pour into prepared pastry shell. Microwave at 5 for 20 to 23 minutes, or until set (center will remain slightly soft). Let stand for at least 30 minutes.

# Graham Cracker Crust

TOTAL COOKING TIME: 5 minutes
Makes 9-in. crust

- ⅓ cup butter or margarine
- 1½ cups finely crushed graham cracker crumbs
- 2 tablespoons sugar

Place butter in 9-in. pie plate. Microwave at HIGH for 1½ to 1¾ minutes, or until butter melts. Add crumbs and sugar; toss to coat. Press mixture firmly against bottom and sides of pie plate. Microwave at 7 for 2½ minutes, turning after half the time.

## Cookie Crumb Crust

Follow the recipe above, substituting vanilla wafer, chocolate wafer or gingersnap crumbs for graham cracker crumbs.

# Tangy Lemon Pie ↑

TOTAL COOKING TIME: 8 minutes
Makes 9-in. pie

- 1 microwaved 9-in. Graham Cracker Crust
- 1 pkg. (3¼ oz.) lemon pudding and pie filling mix
- ¾ cup sugar, divided
- 1¾ cups water
- ¼ cup lemon juice
- 2 eggs, separated
- 1 teaspoon grated lemon peel
- 1 pkg. (3 oz.) cream cheese, cut into chunks

Prepare pie crust as directed, right. Cool. In large bowl blend pudding mix, ½ cup sugar, the water, lemon juice and egg yolks. Microwave at 8 for 5½ to 8 minutes, or until thickened, stirring 2 times. Add lemon peel and cream cheese, beating until blended. Cool.

Beat egg whites until foamy. Gradually add remaining ¼ cup sugar; beating until stiff peaks form. Fold beaten egg whites into cooled filling. Pour into prepared crust. Chill thoroughly. Garnish with lemon slices, if desired.

# Boston Cream Pie ↑

Code: D-1 Medium, D-4 Warm

TOTAL COOKING TIME: 16½ minutes

Makes 9-in. cake

1 pkg. (9 oz.) yellow cake mix

FILLING:

⅓ cup granulated sugar
2 tablespoons cornstarch
⅛ teaspoon salt
1 cup milk
1 egg yolk, slightly beaten
1 tablespoon butter or margarine
¾ teaspoon vanilla

GLAZE:

1 square (1 oz.) unsweetened chocolate
1 tablespoon plus 1 teaspoon butter
    or margarine
½ cup powdered sugar
¼ teaspoon vanilla
1 tablespoon hot water

Line bottom of 9-in. cake dish with wax paper. Prepare cake mix as directed on package. Pour into prepared dish. Microwave at 7 for 5 minutes, turning once. Increase power to HIGH. Microwave for 2½ to 4 minutes, or until center springs back when touched lightly. Let stand for 5 minutes on counter. Invert onto serving plate. Set aside.

In 1-qt. casserole blend granulated sugar, cornstarch and salt. Stir in milk. Microwave at 8 for 3½ to 4½ minutes, or until thickened, stirring 2 times. Stir small amount of hot mixture into egg yolk.

Return to hot mixture. Microwave at 8 for 1 to 1½ minutes, or until thickened. Stir in butter and vanilla. Cool. Split cake in half to make two layers. Spread filling on top of one layer. Top with remaining cake. Cover and refrigerate until filling is firm.

In small bowl microwave chocolate and butter at 7 for 1 to 1½ minutes, or until chocolate softens. Stir to melt chocolate completely. Mix in powdered sugar and vanilla. Stir in hot water, 1 teaspoon at a time, until glaze is desired consistency. Spread glaze over top of cake, allowing to drizzle down side. Cover and chill before serving.

# Black Forest Cake

Code: D-1 Medium
TOTAL COOKING TIME: 16 minutes
Makes 2-layer cake

- 1  **pkg. (19½ oz.) chocolate cake mix**
- 3  **eggs**
- ¾  **cup water**
- ¼  **cup vegetable oil**
- 1  **can (21 oz.) cherry pie filling, divided**
- 1  **teaspoon almond extract**
    **Sifted powdered sugar**

Line bottoms of two 9-in. cake dishes with wax paper. In large mixer bowl combine cake mix, eggs, water and oil. Beat on low speed of electric mixer until moistened, scraping bowl constantly. Beat at medium speed 2 minutes, scraping bowl occasionally. Reserve 1 cup cherry pie filling. Stir remaining pie filling and almond extract into cake batter. Divide between prepared dishes.

Microwave one layer at a time. Place cake dish on inverted saucer and microwave at ⑦ for 5 minutes, turning dish after half the time. Turn dish again after microwaving. Increase power to HIGH. Microwave for 2 to 3 minutes, or until center springs back when touched lightly. Let stand on counter for 5 minutes. Invert onto serving plate. Cool. Repeat with second layer. Spread first layer with reserved pie filling. Top with second cake layer. Sprinkle with powdered sugar before serving.

# Graham Streusel Brunch Cake

Code: D-1 Medium
TOTAL COOKING TIME: 8½ minutes
Makes 9-in. brunch cake

- 1  **cup graham cracker crumbs**
- ⅓  **cup packed brown sugar**
- ⅓  **cup chopped nuts**
- 1  **teaspoon ground cinnamon**
- ⅓  **cup butter or margarine**
- 1  **pkg. (9 oz.) yellow cake mix**

GLAZE:
- ½  **cup powdered sugar**
- 1  **tablespoon milk**

Line bottom of 9-in. cake dish with wax paper. In small bowl combine graham cracker crumbs, brown sugar, nuts, cinnamon and butter. Microwave at HIGH for 1 minute. Stir to blend. Spread half of streusel mixture in prepared dish.

Prepare cake mix as directed on package. Pour half of batter into dish. Top with remaining streusel mixture, then remaining batter. Microwave at ⑦ for 5 minutes; turn dish. Increase power to HIGH. Microwave for 1½ to 2½ minutes, or until center springs back when touched lightly. Let stand for 5 minutes. Invert onto serving plate. Blend powdered sugar and milk. Drizzle over cake.

## *How to Microwave Layer Cakes*

**Mix** cake according to package or recipe directions. Pour into cake dish lined on bottom with wax paper. Microwave one dish at ⑦ for 5 minutes. Turn dish.

**Microwave** at HIGH until top springs back when touched lightly, turning dish once.

**Let stand** on counter for 5 minutes. Invert onto serving plate. Repeat with remaining layer(s).

# Carrot Cake ↑

Code: D-1 Medium
TOTAL COOKING TIME: 20½ minutes
Makes 2-layer cake

- 1½ cups all-purpose flour
- 1½ cups granulated sugar
- 2 teaspoons ground cinnamon
- 1 teaspoon baking powder
- ¾ teaspoon salt
- ½ teaspoon baking soda
- 1 cup vegetable oil
- 3 eggs
- 2 cups grated carrots
- 1 can (8 oz.) crushed pineapple, drained

FROSTING:

- ¼ cup butter or margarine
- 1 pkg. (3 oz.) cream cheese
- 2 cups powdered sugar, divided
- 1 teaspoon vanilla

Line bottoms of two 9-in. cake dishes with wax paper. In large bowl combine flour, sugar, cinnamon, baking powder, salt and baking soda. Mix in oil and eggs. Stir in carrots and drained pineapple. Divide batter between prepared dishes.

Microwave one dish at a time at 7 for 5 minutes, turning dish after half the time. Increase power to HIGH. Microwave for 3 to 5 minutes, or until center springs back when touched lightly, turning 2 times. Let stand on counter for 5 minutes. Invert onto serving plate. Repeat with remaining layer; cool.

Place butter and cream cheese in small bowl. Microwave at HIGH for 30 seconds to soften. Blend. Stir in 1 cup powdered sugar and the vanilla until smooth. Mix in remaining powdered sugar. Spread frosting between layers and on top of cake.

# Apple Cake

Code: D-1 Medium
TOTAL COOKING TIME: 28¼ minutes
Makes 3-layer cake

- 2 cups all-purpose flour
- 1½ cups granulated sugar
- ½ cup packed brown sugar
- 2 teaspoons baking soda
- 1 teaspoon salt
- 1 teaspoon ground cinnamon
- 3 eggs, beaten
- ½ cup vegetable oil
- 1 teaspoon vanilla
- 6 cups chopped, peeled apples (5 to 6 medium)
- 1 cup chopped walnuts

MAPLE FROSTING:

- ¼ cup butter or margarine
- ½ cup dairy sour cream
- ½ teaspoon maple flavoring
- 4 cups powdered sugar

Line bottoms of three 9-in. cake dishes with wax paper. In large bowl combine flour, granulated sugar, brown sugar, baking soda, salt and cinnamon. Blend in eggs, oil and vanilla. Stir in apples and walnuts. Divide batter evenly among prepared dishes. Microwave one layer at a time at 7 for 5 minutes. Turn dish. Microwave at HIGH for 3 to 4 minutes, or until center springs back when touched lightly, turning dish once. Let stand on counter for 5 minutes. Invert onto serving plate. Repeat with remaining layers. Cool.

Place butter in medium bowl. Microwave at HIGH for 1¼ to 1½ minutes, or until butter melts. Blend in sour cream and maple flavoring. Add powdered sugar, 1 cup at a time, mixing until smooth. Spread frosting between layers and on top and sides of cooled cake.

105

# Vanilla Pudding

Code: D-4 Medium
TOTAL COOKING TIME: 9½ minutes
Serves 4 to 6

- ½ cup sugar
- 1 tablespoon plus 2 teaspoons cornstarch
- ⅛ teaspoon salt
- 2 cups milk
- 1 egg, beaten
- 1 tablespoon butter or margarine
- 1 teaspoon vanilla

In 1½-qt. casserole mix sugar, cornstarch and salt. Stir in milk. Microwave at 8 for 6 to 8 minutes, or until thickened, stirring once. Blend small amount of hot mixture into beaten egg. Return to hot mixture. Microwave at 8 for 1 to 1½ minutes, or until thickened, stirring once. Stir in butter and vanilla until butter melts. Pour into serving dishes. Serve warm or chilled.

## Chocolate Pudding

Follow the recipe above, substituting 2 squares (1 oz. each) semi-sweet chocolate for butter.

# Tapioca Pudding

Code: D-4 Medium
TOTAL COOKING TIME: 10 minutes
Serves 6

- 2 cups milk
- 2 eggs, separated
- ⅓ cup sugar, divided
- 2 tablespoons quick-cooking tapioca
- ¼ teaspoon salt
- 1 teaspoon vanilla

In 1½-qt. casserole combine milk, egg yolks, ¼ cup sugar, tapioca and salt; let stand for 5 minutes. Microwave at 8 for 8 to 10 minutes, or until mixture comes to a full boil, stirring frequently. Stir in vanilla. Beat egg whites until foamy. Gradually add remaining sugar; beating until soft peaks form. Fold tapioca mixture into egg whites gently but thoroughly. Spoon into serving dishes. Chill before serving.

# Rice Pudding

TOTAL COOKING TIME: 12½ minutes
Serves 4 to 6

- 2 cups milk
- 2 eggs, beaten
- ½ cup sugar
- ½ teaspoon ground nutmeg
  Dash salt
- ½ teaspoon vanilla
- ⅔ cup uncooked instant rice
- ½ cup raisins

Pour milk into 2-cup measure. Microwave at HIGH for 2½ to 3½ minutes, or until scalded but not boiling. In 1½-qt. casserole blend eggs, sugar, nutmeg, salt and vanilla. Blend in milk, rice and raisins. Microwave at 5 for 8 to 9 minutes, or until thickened, stirring every 2 minutes. Sprinkle with additional nutmeg, if desired. Serve warm or chilled.

# Egg Custard

TOTAL COOKING TIME: 19 minutes
Serves 4

- 1½ cups milk
- ¼ cup sugar
- ¾ teaspoon vanilla
- ¼ teaspoon salt
- 3 eggs
  Dash ground nutmeg

Pour milk into 2-cup measure. Microwave at HIGH for 3½ to 4 minutes, or until scalded but not boiling. In 1½-qt. casserole beat sugar, vanilla, salt and eggs. Gradually stir hot milk into egg mixture. Sprinkle with nutmeg. Cover with wax paper. Microwave at 3 for 11 to 15 minutes, or until custard is set (center will remain slightly soft), turning ¼ turn every 3 minutes. Custard becomes firm as it cools. Chill before serving.

## Apricot Crumble Bars

TOTAL COOKING TIME: 12 minutes
Makes 20 bars

  1  **cup packed brown sugar**
  ¾  **cup butter or margarine**
1½  **cups all-purpose flour**
1½  **cups quick-cooking oats**
  ½  **teaspoon salt**
  1  **jar (12 oz.) apricot preserves (about 1 cup)**

In medium bowl beat brown sugar and butter until creamy. Mix in flour, oats and salt. Reserve 1 cup. Press remaining mixture into buttered 8 × 8-in. baking dish.

Microwave at 7 for 6 to 7 minutes, or until puffy, rotating 2 times. Spread preserves evenly over baked base. Sprinkle reserved mixture evenly over preserves. Microwave at 7 for 5 minutes. Cool. Cut into 20 bars, about 2 × 1½ inches each.

## Frosted Oatmeal Bars

TOTAL COOKING TIME: 7 minutes
Makes 16 bars

  2  **cups quick-cooking oats**
  ½  **cup packed brown sugar**
  ½  **cup butter or margarine**
  ½  **cup honey**
  ½  **cup semi-sweet chocolate chips**
  ¼  **cup peanut butter**

In medium bowl combine oats, brown sugar, butter and honey. Microwave at HIGH for 4½ to 5½ minutes, or until bubbly, stirring 2 times. Spread in 8 × 8-in. baking dish. Cool.

In small bowl combine chocolate chips and peanut butter. Microwave at HIGH for 1 to 1½ minutes, or until chocolate chips are soft, stirring once. Stir and spread over oatmeal base. Cool. Cut into 16 squares, about 2 inches each.

## Ting-a-lings

TOTAL COOKING TIME: 2½ minutes
Makes 2 to 2½ dozen

  1  **pkg. (6 oz.) butterscotch chips**
  ½  **cup peanut butter**
  4  **cups corn flakes, coarsely crushed**
  ½  **cup salted peanuts**

In large bowl combine butterscotch chips and peanut butter. Microwave at 7 for 1½ to 2½ minutes, or until melted, stirring every 30 seconds. Add corn flakes and peanuts. Stir until coated. Drop by rounded teaspoonfuls onto wax paper. Chill until set.

## Chocolate Nut Balls

TOTAL COOKING TIME: 2 minutes
Makes 3 to 3½ dozen

  1  **pkg. (6 oz.) semi-sweet chocolate chips**
  1  **can (5⅓ oz.) evaporated milk**
2½  **cups crushed vanilla wafers**
  ½  **cup powdered sugar**
  2  **tablespoons rum**
1⅓  **cups finely chopped walnuts, divided**

In large bowl combine chocolate chips and evaporated milk. Microwave at 7 for 1½ to 2 minutes, or until chocolate chips melt. Stir in crushed wafers, sugar, rum and ⅓ cup walnuts. Mix thoroughly. Refrigerate for 30 minutes to cool. Shape into balls about 1½ inches in diameter. Roll in remaining walnuts to coat. Chill.

Pictured left to right: Apricot Crumble Bars, Ting-a-lings, Frosted Oatmeal Bars, Chocolate Nut Balls, Mint Fudge

## Mint Fudge

TOTAL COOKING TIME: 12 minutes
Makes 3 pounds

3 cups sugar
1 can (5⅓ oz.) evaporated milk
¾ cup butter or margarine
1 pkg. (12 oz.) semi-sweet chocolate chips
1 jar (7 oz.) marshmallow cream
¼ teaspoon peppermint extract

In 3-qt. casserole combine sugar, evaporated milk and butter. Microwave at 7 for 12 minutes, stirring occasionally. Stir in chocolate chips until melted. Add marshmallow cream and peppermint extract, beating until blended. Pour into buttered 12 × 8-in. baking dish. Chill until set. Cut into squares.

## Bittersweet Chocolate Fondue

TOTAL COOKING TIME: 4½ minutes
Makes about 2½ cups

1 pkg. (12 oz.) semi-sweet chocolate chips
2 squares (1 oz. each) unsweetened chocolate
1 cup half and half
1 teaspoon vanilla
Cake or fruit pieces

In medium bowl combine chocolate chips, unsweetened chocolate, half and half and vanilla. Microwave at 7 for 3 to 4½ minutes, or until chocolate melts, stirring 2 times. Serve with cake or fruit pieces.

109

# Index

110